The Digital Age on the Couc

C000138988

The Digital Age is on the couch. Working today, it is essential that clinicians understand the world we live in. The transition from an industrial economy to an information economy impacts not just the external structure of society and commerce, but also the internal psychic economies of our brains and, inevitably, how clinicians conceptualise the analytic setting in which they practice as therapists and analysts.

The Digital Age on the Couch seeks to understand more about how new technologies interact with the prerogatives of an individual's internal world, how they may alter the psychic structure itself in fundamental ways and the implications this may have for the individual's functioning and for the operation of society. This book attempts, from the perspective of a working clinician, to make some sense of this. The impact of mediation via technology and the consequent disintermediation of the body represent central themes throughout, as they impact on the experience of embodiment, on the 'work of desire' and on the way new media influences psychoanalytic practice.

New media offer opportunities for increasing accessibility to mental health care, including psychoanalytic interventions. However, this requires a sophisticated understanding of how to best create and safeguard the analytic setting. Alessandra Lemma here guides the clinician through an exploration of the limitations and risks of mediated psychotherapy, illustrated with clinical examples throughout.

The Digital Age on the Couch offers an accessibly written guide to combining existing psychoanalytic theory and practice with the challenges presented by digital media. It will appeal to psychoanalysts, psychoanalytic psychotherapists and counsellors.

Alessandra Lemma Alessandra Lemma is a Fellow of the British Psychoanalytical Society and Consultant – Clinical Psychologist at the Anna Freud National Centre for Children and Families. She is Honorary Professor of Psychological Therapies at the School of Health and Human Sciences at Essex University and Visiting Professor, Psychoanalysis Unit, University College London where she is also the Clinical Director of the Psychological Interventions and 'Centro Winnicot', Rome. She is the Editor of the *New Library of Psychoanalysis* book series (Routledge) and one of the regional Editors for the *International Journal of Psychoanalysis*. She has published extensively on psychoanalysis, the body and trauma.

The Digital Age on the Couch

Psychoanalytic Practice and New Media

Alessandra Lemma

Routledge
Taylor & Francis Group

LONDON AND NEW YORK

First published 2017
by Routledge
2 Park Square, Milton Park, Abingdon, Oxon OX14 4RN

and by Routledge
711 Third Avenue, New York, NY 10017

Routledge is an imprint of the Taylor & Francis Group, an informa business

© 2017 Alessandra Lemma

The right of Alessandra Lemma to be identified as author of this work
has been asserted by her in accordance with sections 77 and 78 of the
Copyright, Designs and Patents Act 1988.

All rights reserved. No part of this book may be reprinted or
reproduced or utilised in any form or by any electronic, mechanical, or
other means, now known or hereafter invented, including photocopying
and recording, or in any information storage or retrieval system, without
permission in writing from the publishers.

Trademark notice: Product or corporate names may be trademarks or
registered trademarks, and are used only for identification and
explanation without intent to infringe.

British Library Cataloguing in Publication Data
A catalogue record for this book is available from the British Library

Library of Congress Cataloging in Publication Data
A catalog record for this book has been requested

ISBN: 978-0-415-79112-0 (hbk)
ISBN: 978-0-415-79113-7 (pbk)
ISBN: 978-1-315-21252-4 (ebk)

Typeset in Times New Roman
by Cenveo Publisher Services

To Andy, Matteo, Venetia, Olivia and Tom

Contents

Acknowledgements   ix

Introduction: This modern life   1

PART I
Outside in   II

1   Imagined embodiments, lived embodiments   13
2   The black mirror: Becoming sexual in the digital age   41
3   The disintermediation of desire: From 3D(esire) to 2D(esire)   65

PART II
Inside out   79

4   Mediated psychotherapy   81
5   Digital transference and the therapist's anonymity   114

Conclusion   135
References   141
Index   153

Acknowledgements

For me writing is always the outcome of a curious combination of a most solitary activity and of lively exchange with people who help me to discover what I am thinking. My most constant, enlivening companion on this writing journey has been my husband, Andy, whose knowledge of this particular subject was the added bonus alongside his characteristic curiosity about everything. I am deeply indebted to him for his unstinting support.

I would also like to thank Heather Wood and Linda Young for their helpful comments on an earlier draft and for their generous friendship.

Finally, as ever, I want to thank my patients for their kind permission to make use of our work in this book and for helping me to begin to make sense of the world around us. Where session process detail is provided the individuals concerned have given their consent to its publication. Where there is only descriptive material the cases have been adequately disguised in order to protect confidentiality.

Introduction
This modern life

When I want to understand the anxieties of a particular age I always turn to the most reliable source: jokes. What we laugh about is the best barometer of what troubles us as individuals and as societies.

As I scanned the jokes out there now about the Internet and new technologies they soon became repetitive. Why? Because they merely reworked from different angles what appear to be two prescient preoccupations: the way new media have the potential to remove us from, or replace altogether, actual embodied relationships and the way they can provide an alternative to reality *tout court*.

One joke goes like this:

> – *You know, I have Google+, Facebook, Twitter, Skype accounts ...*
> – *Man, and do you have a life?*
> – *OMG, No! Could you send me a link?*

Another ...

> *A cartoon shows a woman looking angry sitting by her laptop tearing up piles of paper. Her partner comes in and asks: 'What are you doing!' to which she replies: 'I am printing out all the emails you sent me telling me you loved me so I can tear them up!'*

And finally ...

> *A computer programmer happens across a frog in the road. The frog pipes up, 'I'm really a beautiful princess and if you kiss me, I'll stay with you for a week.' The programmer shrugs his shoulders and puts the frog in his pocket. A few minutes later, the frog says 'OK, OK, if you kiss me, I'll give you great sex for a week.' The programmer nods*

and puts the frog back in his pocket. A few minutes later, 'Turn me back into a princess and I'll give you great sex for a whole year!' The programmer smiles and walks on. Finally, the frog says, 'What's wrong with you? I've promised you great sex for a year from a beautiful princess and you won't even kiss a frog?' 'I'm a programmer,' he replies; 'I don't have time for sex ... But a talking frog is pretty neat.'

Network culture

The Digital Age is on the couch. Working today as clinicians, especially if we work with adolescents, requires that we understand the world we live in. External reality may be insufficient to explain internal reality but it is necessary to understand its pressures and trends so as to make sense of how it is then interpreted idiosyncratically.

Every technological revolution coincides with changes in what it means to be a human being, in the kinds of psychological borders that divide the inner life from the world outside. The changes in the way we relate to ourselves and to others do not correspond exactly to the changes in technology: many aspects of today's digital world were already taking shape before the age of the personal computer and the smartphone. But the rapid growth in development, accessibility and use of mobile phones and the Internet suddenly increased the rate and scale of change in all our lives.

Some of these changes can stir disquiet. Perhaps there was similar angst at the birth of the printing press. I was among those who wanted to believe the Internet represented a shift in scale or form, rather than in kind: emails would be the same as letters, only quicker. But increasingly, it seems, that was to underestimate the nature of these developments. The printing press promoted an explosion in the availability of written materials democratising access to information. Now we have gone even further: there are more individual bits of data in cyberspace than there are stars in outer space (Law, 2016). Between 2000 and 2015 the number of people who can access the Internet increased from 6.5 per cent to 43 per cent of the global population (Aiken, 2016). The magnitude of what we have to understand is indeed noteworthy. For example, it is estimated that 38 per cent of Internet users throughout the world use Facebook. If you consider this in relation to our estimated 7 billion world population, Facebook represents 12 per cent of it. In other words if Facebook were a nation it would be the third largest in the world (Law, 2013). The Internet is the biggest thing that human being has created: we all contribute to it every day if only through the data we supply to it (Law, 2016).

The changes we are witnessing reach into every corner of our lives. Once it looked like hype but the Internet really has changed the world completely – and we need to understand how it is changing us along with it. We now routinely do things that just five years ago would scarcely have made sense to us. We tweet along to reality shows; we share videos of cats doing funny things; we communicate while sitting on the toilet (what is colloquially referred to as 'turfing'). It's hard to think of a single human function that technology hasn't somehow altered, apart perhaps from some basic bodily functions such as burping. That's pretty much all we have left. The body is our anchor but even many aspects of our embodied experience can now be altered in dramatic ways through technology. Even urinating has been altered: a 2013 survey found that three-quarters of people now use their mobile phones while sitting on the toilet and that a quarter of men choose to sit on the toilet rather than stand so that they can freely use their phones (Sony and O2, 2013). Technology shapes human behaviour.

In order to understand these modern times it is helpful to keep in mind two key features of current digital life as opposed to the earlier innovations such as desk computing, telephone and television. First, technology is now not primarily about an enhancement of entertainment: it is about a new form of social connectivity. Second, it is a *portable* form of connectivity – a kind of prosthetic that, as Freud (1930) reminds us, affords human being the feeling of being like a 'prosthetic God'. The with-me-everywhere-anytime nature of technology and new media is a new phenomenon that embeds these prosthetics at the very heart of relating and of embodied experience.

In the face of our proliferating representations and reproductions, we need take a second look at ourselves, at how we relate and at how we practise as clinicians. Through the advent of new technologies the real and virtual worlds have begun to merge into a new entity, that is for the current generation digital networks are increasingly an augmentation of the real world rather than an alternative to it (Coleman, 2011). Virtual geographies are an expanded terrain from which experience may be instantly drawn. Simulating presence has also become a standard aspect of how we engage with one another.

This generation is growing up in a network culture where the most superficial and the most intimate forms of relationship include mediation – that is we spend increasing amounts of time engaged in disembodied relating. At a very basic level I am sure that like me you will discover, for example, that there are now people in your life who you know reasonably well, if not very well, whose handwriting you have never seen or not seen enough to recognise it because we hand-write very infrequently. Writing to another person used be to the old fashioned mediated form of communication. It was nevertheless a visceral experience whose idiosyncratic outcome – the handwriting – linked us more directly to the person who wrote to us or to whom we wrote than the impersonal typescript of a text or email. Yes, you can customise and choose your font, but this is not the same experi-ence as your hand touching the piece of paper, as the traces of your skin on the paper as you rest your hand on it, as the odour that can accompany different kinds of paper or as the pressure you may or may not exert when you press the pencil into the paper that will eventually then be held in the hands of its recipient. Clicking a button is a motoric experience, yes, but it is once removed compared to hand-writing. The impact of mediation via technology and the consequent disintermediation of the body represent central themes in my thinking throughout this book as they impact on the experience of embodi-ment, on the 'work of desire' and on how we practise as clinicians.

About this book

The transition from an industrial economy to an information economy impacts not just the external structure of society and commerce, but also internal psychic economies (Guignard, 2014), our brains (Greenfield, 2014) and, of course, how we conceptualise the analytic setting in which we practise as therapists and analysts. We need to understand more about how these new technologies interact with the prerogatives of an individu-al's internal world, how they may alter psychic structure itself in funda-mental ways and the implications of this for the individual's functioning and also for how a society operates. This book is an attempt, from the perspective of a working clinician, to make some sense of this. It is not intended to be exhaustive in its consideration of the impact of new tech-nology/media on theory or practice. It is, in fact, quite concise because it reflects an admittedly selective and focused examination of the impact of digital media on the experience of embodiment and sexuality, which have long been of interest to me. It is a distillation of my personal learning as a therapist and analyst working in digital times in the hope that this expe-rience can be of help to clinicians trying to work psychoanalytically at this particular point in time. As Gabbard observes, we are confronted with a challenge:

> We cannot turn back time. We cannot rewind the videotape. Perhaps we can find creative ways of adapting to the brave new world we are encountering … There is no question that we are in the path of a juggernaut that will crush any opposition that arises. So we should probably go along for the ride and see where it leads us rather than begin our journey with the dinosaurs towards extinction. (2015: 540)

Writing about the digital age, however, is a daunting task. As I write this book new technological developments are underway and adding further layers to the so-called 'new' that render the 'now' already redundant. My thoughts and my typing fingers are not fast enough to keep up with the very changes I am writing about. It is easy to be seduced into believing that we need to think faster in order to think better and to keep up with the times. The speed of change, and the speed that this technological revolution has embedded at the core of contemporary Western and non-Western cultures, is unprecedented. Speed is now woven into the very fabric of our lives within and outside of the consulting rooms we practise in as therapists and analysts.

It could be argued, with some justification, that psychoanalysis as a discipline needed to speed up to keep apace with the changing times in order to remain relevant to contemporary culture. In the current climate, however, it is important to also pause for breath and draw on one of its key tenets: absence, waiting, gaps – all of which march to a slower tempo – may be painful and frustrating, and their toleration should not be fetishised as the path to mental health, but these are essential experiences that push us towards the vital psychic task of representation.

Speed introduces a tension between presentation and representation. On a daily basis we are 'presented' with numerous images and sound bytes. The world afar is presented to us via various media that collapse space into time. This constant feeding means that we have on tap unprecedented access to knowledge that can expand the mind. At the same time in order for the mind to develop the emotional resilience required to process experience the mind needs to have space – *an absence of presentation* – that impels it to represent experience. This, as I shall suggest in this book, is necessary for the successful integration of mind and body, for sustaining the necessary 'work of desire' and for the development of sexuality during adolescence.

In Part 1 'Outside In' I am primarily concerned with how the external world impacts on the subjective experience of embodiment (Chapter 1) and more specifically on sexual development during adolescence (Chapter 2). I also examine how the 'work' of desire is being shaped by new technologies and I illustrate this through the use of Spike Jonze's film *Her* (Chapter 3).

In Part II 'Inside Out' I am primarily concerned with the way new media have impacted on psychoanalytic practice. New media offer opportunities for increasing accessibility to mental health care including psychoanalytic interventions (Scharff, 2013; Lemma and Fonagy, 2013. However, this requires a sophisticated understanding of how to best create and safeguard the analytic setting and we have much to learn in this respect. Anyone engaging with this medium for the delivery of therapy needs to be well acquainted with its significant limitations and risks, which I outline in Chapters 4 and 5 and explore through clinical examples.

Four key assumptions guide my thinking about the digital age and the technological developments it promotes:

1   The developments under discussion are not intrinsically good or bad but neither are they neutral, as Kranzberg (1986) suggested.
2   These developments can sometimes support analytic work either through the medium they provide for distance therapy, with all its many caveats, but also through the use made by the patient of the 'space' new media provide for the elaboration of bodily and psychic experience.
3   However, by virtue of some of modern technology's key characteristics, new media also provide the theatre, par excellence, for the acting out of many neurotic and perverse conflicts.
4   In all likelihood the pervasiveness of the changes brought about by new media is likely to impact on psychic structure and hence on how we relate to each other in our intimate, familial and social relationships.

What does all this mean for psychoanalysis? It means that it needs to review some of its theories and practice to accommodate the implications of these changes. This need not lead to changes – in fact it may lead to reasserting key psychoanalytic tenets. But the process of review is nevertheless necessary in order to engage with these changes. Standing still and protecting the analytic fort has not served well our discipline in the past. It will not serve it well now either.

Of course what I write about in this book is from the possibly distorted perspective of a Digital Immigrant. But I am one who has nevertheless specialised for many years in working with the popularly dubbed Digital Natives of a changed communication landscape that is still evolving and only partially understood. I hope this allows me to sustain a balanced of view of technological developments that act as a canvas on which we tend to project our hopeful and pessimistic views of humanity and society.

The changing landscape of the clinical problems I have seen over thirty years of practice spanning pre- and post-Internet times leads me to wonder about how technological advances may be shaping the development of the mind and its vicissitudes. My experience of working with adolescents has been very important in shaping my thinking and several of the clinical examples are drawn from my work with adolescents and young adults. This work has given me some interesting snapshots of the psychic opportunities and risks that bear on young people today and the part that new technology and media appear to play in this respect.

New technologies and media, however, do not create new problems per se. Rather they provide new theatres for the enactment of internal world dynamics. By virtue of their particular contingencies new technologies and media can lead to a rapid escalation of enactments, as I discuss in Chapter 5, or it can become very addictive for some people as is most apparent when we consider Internet pornography (Wood, 2014) (see also Chapter 2, this book).

With each shifting automation, simulation and transmission we discover not only new technologies but also new facets of ourselves. Our modes of communication impact our concepts of space, place and time, such that as we change modalities of representation we also change our human perspective. This raises both possibilities for constructive change and progress as well as for evasion into psychic retreats (Steiner, 1993), that is a psychic withdrawal from reality that can now be inhabited in virtual space. As Birksted-Breen aptly put it:

> The individual is forever looking to achieve non-recognition of aspects of himself through splitting, denial, disavowal, repression and projection, while also looking to achieve coherence. (2016: 50)

It is therefore important to consider not what technology 'causes' as such but rather what risks it presents at the individual and social level, though consideration of the latter is beyond the scope of this book.

I personally have many questions about the impact of new technologies and especially the domain of cyberspace on psychic structure but I am quite clear about one thing: communication technologies ought to be of great interest to contemporary psychoanalytic practitioners. The very existence of communication networks that facilitate and regulate intimacy, with varying degrees of connection and disconnection, strikes at the heart of what we painstakingly try to understand with our patients in our daily practices: how to manage being-with-self-and-others. In so far as these technologies have the potential to perform such important psychic functions, it is incumbent on us to distinguish between the 'properties of tools' and 'what people do with them' (Chartier, 1997: 11). In this book I therefore make a clear distinction between the potential constructive use of technology in the context of a therapeutic process where both patient and therapist are physically present (see Chapter 1) and the use of new media to deliver psychotherapy (see Chapter 4).

Technological developments are 'developments' in the sense that they have created opportunities for extending learning and creativity and they may be used by some individuals to assist developmental processes. It is incumbent on us as clinicians to be receptive to the possibility that technological developments can be used to support psychic development as much as they can be used to foreclose experience. This has obvious technical implications in terms of how we approach in our interpretations the patient's use of new technologies to meet the prerogatives of the internal world.

How technique has been affected (or not) by the phenomena of a changing world is a prescient question. While analysts and therapists are now finally writing about this there is, in my view, an urgent need for more discussion and reflection on our changing practice that is rooted in the clinical reality of our day-to-day practice. 'Technique' may not quite capture what I have in mind when I think about what needs to change in our daily practice in response to this 'changing world', if by technique we mean when or whether to make transference interpretations or whether we use the couch or not, for example. What needs to change primarily in order to accommodate the changing world is our willingness to engage with these cultural changes and with other disciplines that can help us to understand these changes, and to be open to how this may require us to revisit cherished assumptions. This will include how we do things (i.e. technique), but not only. Our 'internal setting' needs to change too so that we can be specifically attuned to how growing up and living in these times of technoculture may require us to focus more closely on certain aspects of our patient's experiences that are directly affected by new technologies, not least the experience of embodiment and sex.

When discussing the impact of technology on the psyche we must be wary of generalisations. The mind is a complex apparatus charged, as it were, from within (internal reality) and from without (external reality) in addition to any constitutional endowments. No aspect of external reality impacts in a linear way on internal reality; rather, it is modified by the highly idiosyncratic filter that is internal reality.

Inevitably in this book I can only share personal speculations. In so doing I am mindful that our clinic-based observations are necessarily skewed in the direction of pathology and that this, in isolation, is not a valid basis for formulating so-called normal development. To complicate matters, however, it is still too early to draw any conclusions because these developments are still relatively new. At the time of writing this book the Internet, for public use, has only been in existence for almost twenty-five years. As such what I write stands as a snapshot of these modern times as they are *now* based on what I have experienced as a clinician. Over the next twenty-five years new insights and new developments will emerge and may render what I write obsolete and certainly incomplete.

Part I

Outside in

Man has, as it were, become a kind of prosthetic God. When he puts on all his auxiliary organs he is truly magnificent, but those organs have not grown onto him and they still give him much trouble at times.

(Freud, 1930: 37)

Chapter 1

Imagined embodiments, lived embodiments

When we write we always write at a precise moment in time. What we write will be read at a different point in time by an audience who will be far removed from the spatio-temporal space framing the writer's embodied experience as they wrote. Yet that 'frame' embodies the ideas: it is important as it locates in space and time – and hence in the body – the thoughts that are eventually received by the reader.

So let me share my writing 'frame'. As I sit at my desk and start to write this chapter in London in January 2016, I am filled with images of David Bowie's video, *Lazarus*, released only three days before his death on 10 January 2016. I have downloaded and watched this video several times on my laptop. It compels me and haunts me in equal measure.

The opening scene exposes us to a blindfolded, fragile-looking Bowie lying in bed. Two small buttons over the blindfold serve as his eyes – a reference one assumes to the coins used to pay the ferryman, Charon, for safe passage across the river Styx to get into the underworld of Hades. It becomes clear that Bowie is in a hospital bed. Soon he begins to float above it, signifying his journey towards death, which he was anticipating as he was diagnosed with terminal cancer at the time.

I choose to start this chapter with this reference to Bowie because as I watched this video on my laptop I was struck by the powerful visceral effect on me of images of Bowie's convulsing body and of his music, all received remotely. Yet Bowie's experience of embodiment is anything but 'remote' in the impact it had on me. The images of Bowie's body in the video resonated and evoked actual physical sensations in my body, and reflections on my body and mortality. I could feel my body respond and be altered by the images and music as I projected myself into this sensory experience.

We might say that my experience is as virtual as any experience can be in cyberspace:[1] I was not physically present at the filming of the video or at Bowie's death. I have not even had to use my body to leave the comfort of my house to purchase the video in a shop. I am in control of when, where and how often I choose to download the video. I can conjure up in an instant the version of him that I like best. Bowie is a virtual figure for me – as virtual as any character in a computer game – because Bowie is whatever I have needed him to be for me during my lifetime and at this particular juncture. I am not even wearing any virtual 'gear' to simulate any physical sensations. In the profoundest sense, however, the experience of watching and hearing him in the video is all too real for me at the level of the affects and fantasies it arouses and, importantly, in how this impact is registered and mediated by my body. It changes how I feel in my body and how I feel about it. These changes are real for me. Importantly my relationship with this visual and auditory content, mediated by the computer screen, contributes to changes at the level of my representation of my body in my mind, at least in the short term. The technology and what it permits interacts with my inner world and my body becomes through it.

In Chapters 2 and 3 I will explore some of the more adverse implications of new technological developments. But at core I do not subscribe to a wholly dystopic view of these developments. In this chapter I will suggest that technology and new media present us with as many risks as they do opportunities: what makes the difference is *how* we use them. I will explore the ways in which the way a patient uses technology and new media might afford opportunities *alongside* an analytic process. In particular I will focus on how bodies become through their relations with the multitude of images, representations and visceral experiences that new technologies make possible remotely to suggest that an *imagined embodiment* facilitated by technology and new media may support a constructive psychic developmental process.

Embodiment is a complex process that underlies our relation to the world. Our lived body generates our understanding of the world and of ourselves. Any reconstitution of the body through its interaction with technology and new media will result in a transformation of subjective experience, however temporary or enduring and however helpful or destructive. Psychoanalytic theorising on the body needs to focus not only on how technology/new media effect bodies, but also on how bodies are experienced through technology/new media and on how these experiences may limit or extend the becoming of bodies. To this end I draw on Deleuze's concept of 'becoming' to propose a model for approaching our thinking about the body and technology grounded in process where bodies and technology/new media are not seen as separate entities between which relations operate, but as constituted through their relationship (Coleman, 2011).

The reality of the virtual

A central point of debate in discussions about new technologies concerns whether virtual reality may be considered to be a dimension of the real world or whether in its passive immersion it draws us into a distancing fascination that insulates us from the real (Žižek, 1997b). I want to suggest that virtual reality need not be a literal enactment of Cartesian ontology. Artists and theorists like Monika Fleischmann (2009, cited in Brians (2011)), for example, who are engaged in how the body actually interacts with technologies, have been very helpful in bringing to the fore the fact that even in virtual environments the material body remains relevant. To this end Fleischmann introduced the concept of *mixed reality* – a powerful notion that enables us to consider the body as simultaneously taking part in, and being formed by, both the 'material' and the 'virtual'. Material bodies, their virtual representation, human imagination and computer hardware/software all interact to produce a reality that has both material and virtual elements.

If we take *Second Life* as a working example, like other emerging media technologies of the early twenty-first century that possess the qualities of real-time interactions, visualisation and a sense of inhabiting space together, the virtual world offers everyday users an experience that is neither entirely virtual nor real, but one that has been described by some media theorists as 'virtually actual' (Coleman, 2011).

Any consideration of the virtual has to consider Deleuze's ideas because he is the philosopher of the Virtual par excellence. However, let's be clear: what matters to Deleuze is not virtual reality, but the reality of the virtual. Virtual reality in itself is a rather uninspiring idea as far as he is concerned: that of imitating reality, of reproducing its experience in an artificial medium. The reality of the virtual, on the other hand, stands for the reality of the virtual as such, for its real effects and consequences. If we adopt Deleuze's suggestion that 'the virtual is opposed not to the real but to the actual' (1994: 208) then the virtual is fully real insofar as it is virtual. The virtual here is conceived of as a finite set of potentialities through which some potentialities are actualised (as opposed to an infinite set of potentialities, some of which are realised).

In order to engage theoretically as well as clinically with new technologies we have to move beyond the binary logic of virtual and real, and understand the world we are currently living in. The virtual, as I use the term here, does not substitute the real. Rather it is an attribute of the real, an expression among many of reality. The virtual brings into relief notions such as the possible, the potential, the probable, the fictional. Something is virtual when it exists in an not-as-yet-actualised form.

However, for a discipline like psychoanalysis – one predicated on the fundamental human tension between the lure of the 'pleasure principle' and the dampener of the 'reality principle' (Freud, 1923b) – the virtual is to the real what the copy is to the original: it is a reproduction that allows wishes to colonise reality. This definition of 'virtual' typically stands in opposition to the notion of 'real'. The virtual here is always 'less than' the original. The virtual is seen to omnipotently divest the so-called 'real' of its flesh and bones reality. As such thinking about the nature of virtual reality can become polarised: the virtual becomes equated with 'not authentic', a retreat away from so-called reality. Even though virtual reality *may* be used to effectuate a retreat away from reality – and our clinical everyday practice attests to this – we could equally argue for a notion of a virtuality that is not always about a 'safe copy' of, or 'alternative' to, the 'real'.

Problems arise, of course, from a psychological point of view, when we are no longer thinking in terms of the virtual as a space for experimentation or augmentation but more along the lines of the virtual as alternative to the real (Lemma, 2014). And yet psychoanalysis helps us to also appreciate the fundamental importance of fantasy to psychic survival and development, for better or for worse, and just like fantasy, cyberspace and the kind of virtuality it promotes may represent a necessary step towards the realm of what is possible. In other words, it may contain the seeds for imagining oneself as different and hence at some stage for being different. Here the real may be seen as partial, flawed while the virtual promises a resolution to come, which may then be experimented with in virtual reality before being actualised in reality. To take a recent physical example of this, in a remarkable medical breakthrough, patients left paralysed by severe spinal cord injuries have recovered the ability to move their legs after training with an exoskeleton linked to their brain. The training involved the patients using virtual reality to control a computer avatar with a brain–machine interface. When these individuals thought about walking forward, the avatar would move as if it was their body. They then used the same system to control a robot and finally an exoskeleton that the patients could wear (Johnson, 2016).

Designers, and the code they construct, go a long way toward making a virtual world real. Sometimes they create imaginative scenes only found in science fiction or fantasy but they also help mirror the offline world by creating more straightforward representations of our everyday environments. In each case they significantly provide a means of embodiment for the user. For graphical worlds, this comes in the form of avatars – those pictorial constructs used to actually inhabit the world. It is in large part through these avatars that users can come to bring real life and vibrancy to the spaces. Through avatars, users embody themselves and make real their engagement within a virtual world. Avatars, in fact, come to provide access points in the creation of identity and social life. The bodies people use in these spaces provide a means to live digitally – to fully inhabit that space. It is therefore not simply that users exist as just 'mind', but instead construct their identities through avatars.

Needless to say the detailed and highly specified 'worlds' that can be accessed in cyberspace are in some important respects far removed from reality, not least because reality does not pre-exist in the form of specified representations to be recovered by consciousness. Reality cannot be programmed in advance because the chaotic elements from the many systemic forces that shape our daily lives – not least the unconscious mind – work to produce the generative breakdown from which subjectivity emerges and which we call 'life'. Virtual reality instead functions more like fantasy: as a kind of filter and focus presenting to the mind (and acting on the body) only those details essential for enhancing a specific experience.

The persistence of the flesh

Cyberculture popularised a world where the body becomes redundant or, as the work of body artist Stelarc illustrates, where the body is an empty structure that new technologies can sculpt (Lemma, 2010). In truth, however, virtual bodies have never been virtual if by that we mean non-material. This is why the techno-fantasy of escaping the body in a bodiless cyberspace fails: we are constituted through a dynamic interaction between our biological bodies, their virtual representation and signification, our physical and social environments and the myriad conscious and unconscious processes that produce them.

Paradoxically what is at stake when we consider the body in virtual reality is how it exposes the limits of the body: it does not deny them or render the body obsolete. Rather it confronts the body in its limits. From this standpoint the virtual body puts the real fleshy body into perspective. It is the latter that we all struggle to accommodate into our subjective experience. This brings to mind Kant's dove. Kant observed a dove might think it would find flying easier without the encumbrance of air around it but such a bird would, inevitably, soon discover flight in a vacuum impossible. Like Kant's dove if we deny the fleshy, messy, limited nature of the body we cannot begin to understand who we are.

In the 1990s cyberspace was hailed by some as an arena for the realisation of the disembodied mind: a kind of 'disembodied technocracy' (Gunkel, 1998: 119). From a theoretical point of view, in order to understand what is happening in cyberspace, we need to embrace a less accommodating view of disembodiment. Rather than cyberspace being a place for a pure meeting of minds, the body still matters even when interaction is mediated (Lemma, 2015a). After all, even William Gibson's eponymous cowboy in *Neuromancer* had to hook himself up to a catheter in order to manage extended time in cyberspace (Brians, 2011).

When in cyberspace we are still embodied even if we might choose to deny this to ourselves. What changes is our experience of embodiment because we are no longer dependent on the old contingent relations to the corporeal. This is why we ought to be interested in the reconstruction of bodies online and how these online activities inform, or not as the case may be, one's offline experience of embodiment and hence our sense of identity. Of note in this respect is the fact that we have witnessed a dramatic shift from the World Wide Web as a text-only medium for the first twenty years of its life since Tim Berners-Lee's development, to one that is now increasingly visual. This has important repercussions for our overall experience of embodiment.

The virtual body amounts to a virtual representation of one's self in physical form (e.g. the avatar) that may or may not correspond closely to one's objective body. Nowadays we therefore need to consider the objective body that refers to one's physical form, the virtual body and the body one experiences within immersive environments, that is one's phenomenal experience of embodiment when in cyberspace.

The virtual worlds of cyberspace provide a fresh arena for the staging of the body in which new dramas can be enacted but where perhaps we can also experiment with new or denied or conflicted facets of ourselves that meet with validation by others. Cyberspace offers a multitude of potentially safe spaces for those who are socially anxious to explore who they

are, as well as spaces where those who are unsure of their sexual preferences can explore various aspects of their sexuality. Some individuals
intentionally take on different personas in cyberspace (e.g. gender switch-
ing) in order to be able to express hidden truths about themselves. My aim
in approaching this subject is thus not to demonise the virtual domain.

Body matters

We are naturally prosthetic taking whatever we can from the world. We
have a tendency to mix the biological and the technical – a 'cognitive
hybridization' (Clark, 2003) that allows us to extend our mental and
physical capacities. This was at the core of McLuhan's (1994) definition
of media as extensions of human being:

> All technologies are extensions of our physical and nervous systems to
> increase power and speed. (1994: 90)

And:

> Any extension, whether of skin, hand, or foot, affects the whole psy-
> chic and social complex. (1994: 4)

Thus the wheel extends our feet, the phone extends our voice, television
extends our eyes and ears, the computer extends our brain, and electronic
media, in general, extend our central nervous system.

To understand the relationship between the body and 'tools' I have
found it useful to turn to philosophy. Heidegger's (1962) analysis of tool
use is a case in point. For a tool to be ready-to-hand it must, in Heidegger's
terms, 'withdraw'. In so doing, the tool becomes the means rather than the
object of the experience (Ihde, 1990). This has a parallel with the experience of the body: Sartre (1970) sees the body as the perpetually 'surpassed'
(p. 233). But what Heidegger highlights is how the tool itself is also
surpassed as it withdraws into the architecture of the body, forming 'an
embodiment relation' (Ihde, 1990).

This originary coupling of the human and the technical was also central
to Merleau-Ponty's thinking – a truly extraordinary thinker about the
body, which is why I will dwell a bit on his ideas:

> … to get used to a hat, a car, a stick is to be transplanted into them, or
> conversely to convert them into the bulk of our own body. (1962: 143)

To illustrate his ideas Merleau-Ponty (1962) invokes the example of the blind person's cane. The cane for the blind person is no longer an object, but an extension of the realm of the senses. With the cane as a 'familiar instrument', touch is experienced at its end point: 'its point has become an area of sensitivity' (p. 143), as he put it, rather than at the hand. The incorporation of the tool into the body gestalt is what Leder (1990: 34) refers to as a 'phenomenological osmosis', whereby the body allows instruments to melt into it.[2] Our childrens' bodies, if born within the last ten years or so, will have a body gestalt that is quite different to their parents' generation as smartphones and laptops, for example, will have been accessible to them early on, among other 'toys'. They have become everyday prosthetic extensions of the current generation's body. We thus need to consider how we operate as overlapping systems – digital and non-digital – to create a space that institutes embodiment in a virtual location (Vasseleu, 1997), keeping in mind that technology can never be purely digital and thus a-cultural or a-social or untouched by the unconscious of its developers and users.

Bodily experience has always been conditioned by a technical dimension and has occurred as a co-functioning of embodiment with technologies. Technology, we might say, stimulates the potential of the body to open the world to the self. The mixed reality paradigm that I referred to earlier is very relevant to this discussion because it foregrounds the constitutive role of the body in giving birth to the world:

> The psychical apparatus develops through successive stages of breaking with its biological bases, breaks which on the one hand make it possible to escape from biological laws and on the other make it necessary to look for an anaclitic relationship of every psychical to a bodily function. (Merleau-Ponty, 1962: 96)

This is very resonant with Freud's (1923a) recognition of the importance of the body ego to the development of the self. As Merleau-Ponty recognised, the body is 'a primary access to the world'. What he meant is that the body forms an ultimate background. 'The body', writes Merleau-Ponty, 'operates according to a latent knowledge it has of the world – a knowledge anterior to cognitive experience' (p. 233). 'To have a body', he adds, 'is to possess a universal setting, a schema of all types of perceptual unfolding' (Merleau-Ponty, 1962: 326).

Merleau-Ponty thus emphasised the absolute priority of the phenomenal body and the primary role accorded to bodily motility in the constitution of a systemic coupling between organism and environment. What makes the passage from reality to virtual so seamless is precisely the capacity of our embodied form to create reality through motor activity (this is not specific to cyberspace – that is simply the medium we are discussing now).

Merleau-Ponty's model of embodied intentionality includes a space for the body schema – an anterior condition of the possibility for perception. The body schema refers to the system of sensory-motor processes that constantly regulate posture and movement. It is a 'set of laws rather than images' (Gallagher, 2005). Clinicians tend on the whole to be concerned with the body image – the representation we have of our body in our mind with the attendant affect associated with it. The body image is not innate, and here psychoanalysis can make a valuable contribution in understanding the developmental factors that play a part in shaping and affectively colouring this representation.

It is also important, however, to understand how the body prior to emotional, cognitive and social experience helps to constitute the meaning that comes to consciousness. In other words, the perception of my body already speaks of certain 'dispositions' that I have towards it (beliefs and phantasies) as well as certain 'dispositions' my body has towards the world (a posture, a sense of balance) and other visceral, autonomic aspects of embodiment (Gallagher, 2005).

A more disciplined phenomenology reveals that the body in the world constitutes our locus, so that we are 'here' rather than 'there'. Crucially movement always displaces the self thus preventing it from coinciding with itself: there is always an 'elsewhere', a point that is 'not where I am now' and hence 'other', not within my reach or control. In other words, we first encounter otherness through movement: 'In order that we may be able to move our body towards an object, the object must first exist for it, our body must not belong to the 'in-itself' (Merleau-Ponty 1962: 133).

Here Meleau-Ponty's notion of embodied alterity is important because it underscores why embodiment is so problematic for us all. If I can present his position a little schematically, basically his later philosophy attempts to reinforce that self and other are relationally constituted via their potential reversibility. One example of this might be the way in which looking at another person always also involves the tacit recognition that we too can be looked at. According to Merleau-Ponty (and here he differs from Sartre), we do not simply oscillate between being the looker and being the looked-upon. Instead, he suggests, each experience is betrothed to the other in such a way that we are never simply a disembodied looker. Rather, the alterity of the other's look is always already involved in us.

These ideas are clinically relevant because the notion of embodied alterity reminds us of the fundamental opacity of the other that is at the core of our embodied experience. The unfathomability of the other resides within us. When we compulsively manipulate our embodied experience, and hence the representation of our bodies in our minds, say via virtual technologies, or by modifying the surface of our bodies via cosmetic surgery or tattoos (Lemma, 2010, 2014), we are searching for more or less adaptive ways of managing the otherness inscribed in our bodies.

The body always has to balance two contrary requirements: completeness and self-sufficiency. A body detached from all that is other than itself would be hopelessly incomplete, divorced from the means of its own sustainability. A body must complete itself in order to maintain itself: it must be open to what is not merely itself but this requires relinquishing the mythic self-sufficiency of narcissism. But the desire (or felt necessity) for completeness comes into conflict with self-sufficiency or with the desire to not be exposed to contingency, risk or an influx of otherness. This presents us with a profound challenge that may lead us to manipulate our bodies or try to escape them. And here, of course, new technologies/media provide the new theatres where this can occur with ever greater ease.

Tech theatres of the body and mind

In order to engage with the question of how the body interacts with technology and its impact on us I have found it very helpful to understand bodies as *becomings* and to explore the ways in which bodies become through their interaction with new media: what extensions and limitations of becoming are produced through particular relations between bodies and technology (Coleman, 2011).

The concept of becoming[3] is indebted to the French philosopher, Deleuze.[4] Taking his lead from Nietzsche's early work, Deleuze uses the term 'becoming' (*devenir*) to describe the continual production (or 'return') of difference immanent within the constitution of events, whether physical or otherwise. Becoming is the pure movement evident in changes between particular events. Becoming therefore does not represent a transformation between one state into another. It is not a derivative process that induces identification with or imitating someone in order to become like it. It is not the end-state.[5] Rather, becoming is a force of transformation itself. It is this latter feature that I wish to emphasise above all else as the foundation for my conceptual approach to understanding how patients may use technology to enact embodied psychic experiences – for better or for worse.

For Deleuze, becoming explains the world not as comprising relatively stable and discrete forms or beings (e.g. subjects/objects) but as processes of movement, variation and multiplicity. Identity in this context is revealed not as an essence but as an amalgam of heterogeneous elements that include biological, evolutionary and developmental processes, social and cultural codings and accidents of history.

In highlighting how a body becomes through its interconnections with multiple and diverse things, Deleuze (1994) is arguing that a body is a process that becomes through its relations and, as such, there are no relations between pre-existent entities (e.g. between bodies and technology or between subjects and objects) but rather entities are constituted through their relations (Fraser *et al*. 2005). A body then is not a human subject who has relations with technology; rather, a body is the relation between a human subject and technology.

The articulation of this conceptual stance is not pure pedantry. Rather it helps us to move away from the question of whether technology and new media are 'good' or 'bad' and focus instead on what the relations between bodies and technology may limit or extend. According to this perspective, it is not that using an avatar, as I will shortly illustrate through my work with Jane, for example, has a negative or positive effect on her body image or her gender identifications since within this conceptual framework there are no clear lines of division between them (Coleman, 2011). Instead, the relations between Jane's body and her avatar produce a particular outcome, which in her case appeared to be helpful. However, to argue that bodies become through their relations with technology is not to overlook the ways in which some of our patients may misuse technology to bypass, for example, the meaning of the body for them.

It would be all too easy to find a case that illustrates the use of cyberspace as a defensive retreat and I have dealt with this elsewhere (Lemma, 2011). Instead I now want to turn to some clinical material from two cases – an adolescent girl and an adult male patient – to illustrate how cyberspace may also create the opportunity for the elaboration of an *imagined embodiment* that in contrast to the *lived embodiment* provides the individual with a different experience that can support development.

Jane

Jane was a 17-year-old girl who sought help because her parents became concerned after she cut short her previously long hair and told them that she wanted to be a boy. Jane had never said this before, or even consciously thought it, she told me when we first met. And yet she was now convinced that she was 'trans', that 'being in the wrong body' provided a persuasive account for her long-standing unhappiness and difficulty in establishing a sexual relationship with boys. Around this time a female school friend who had a crush on her declared her attraction to Jane. Even though Jane had not reciprocated she told me that she was keen to explore a homosexual relationship – except that she did not see it as such in her mind now because it was her 'really a boy' self that liked the idea of sex with a girl and hence this was not 'me being a lesbian'.

Jane was profoundly confused about who she was. Now that the idea of being 'trans' had taken hold in her mind she frantically searched the Internet for information about transitioning. In her online gaming her avatar was now a male one. In her day-to-day life she wore androgynous clothes and her hair was kept immaculately short. She had thrown away all her make-up, denigrated her previous 'girlie' self and spent hours (literally) studying YouTube videos of her favourite male YouTubers to 'learn' male mannerisms that she then tried to emulate. She would stand in front of the mirror in her bedroom and practise. Sometimes these 'practice' sessions ended in tears as she thought she could not pass convincingly; at other times she relished being mistaken for a boy in the street only to then feel crushed by the sound of her feminine voice that betrayed her sex to the world.

Jane felt happiest when online because there she said she could be the boy she felt herself to be. Her new male persona (Jake) could 'breathe' online, as she put it, and hence cyberspace became all-consuming, not least because her parents were putting her under considerable pressure to 'come to my senses' and focus instead on her pending exams. Being in cyberspace and relating to others through the medium of technology was her safe retreat from the pressures of reality.

Over time, however, Jane helped me to understand that to view this 'space' as a 'retreat' was not quite right if by retreat we have in mind a place characterised by an absence of working through of conflicts or a place where reality is denied. Instead in cyberspace, and alongside her work in therapy, Jane was working very hard to find out who she was: she was 'playing with reality' to define the contours of her self through finding an embodied form that could guarantee what she felt she lacked.

Jane was an only child born to a teenage mother who had given her up for adoption at birth. She had been adopted into an affluent family that was in many respects stable but both parents seemed rather conservative in their outlook on life. Jane's declaration that she was 'trans' came as a shock to them and they did not feel equipped to deal with this. Her adoptive mother was described as 'kind but weak'. The adoptive father was described as 'conventional and serious' and very successful in his field of work. She told me that her adoptive mother had wanted more children but the father had not agreed because of his work commitments.

A few weeks into the therapy I asked Jane about her biological parents, as she had made no mention at all about them. She was dismissive in her reply, saying that she had no interest in them and that she did not think that her difficulties were connected to being adopted.

I said that she was making it very clear that she did not want me to write off her feeling that she was a boy with some off-the-shelf interpretation about adoption.

She seemed relieved when I said this, adding that she had felt all her life that her problems had been put down to that, but that she was clear that her adoption had nothing to do with anything. She emphasised that she had never been curious about her biological parents. She had been told that her biological mother – who was of Indian origin – had 'difficulties' and could not look after her. She knew nothing about her biological father except that he was British and had not supported the mother when she became pregnant.

After a silence Jane said that her adoptive mother had recently bought a book I had written – 'probably to check you out', she added pointedly – and that when she had picked it up Jane had noticed that I had made a reference in the acknowledgements to a male name whom she presumed to be my son. She was quite sure I must have a son and in fact she imagined I had more than one son. I was struck by the certainty of her assumption as if there could be no place in my mind, or hers, for a girl.

I replied that perhaps she too was trying to 'check me out' and determine if I preferred boys or girls.

'Well do you have a preference?' she then asked provocatively.

I replied that she seemed very preoccupied with what was in my mind about boys and girls and whom I might prefer and what I thought about her decision to become a boy.

'I have not *decided* to become a boy. I am becoming who I should always have been. That's quite different,' she added angrily.

I was struck by her reaction. Yet I felt strangely at ease with how I had phrased what I said since it reflected accurately what I felt: unlike many transsexual young people I have seen who go on to fully transition, Jane's 'trans' identity felt somewhat 'off-the-shelf': no less urgent or meaningful, and surely to be taken seriously, but not the culmination of years of struggle in a sexed body that felt misaligned with her felt-to-be gender identity. I wondered to myself whether the affective kernel of truth lay in her experience of some kind of profound misalignment that left her feeling stranded in a body that could not help her to forge a stable identity. The way she was managing this disturbing internal experience was to label this 'trans' so as to make it tangible in a form that was communicable to others. Nowadays the 'trans' label does act as such a safety net for some young people, a point I shall return to later (see also Chapter 2).

I agreed with Jane that there was a difference but that in fact I had put it that way because, rightly or wrongly, that was how I heard her: that she had 'decided' a few months ago that she was really a boy even though she had never before been concerned about her gender identity. I could also hear that this made her angry and that I hoped she could help me to better understand her position since she seemed to feel I misunderstood her.

Jane said that she had always hated her body and that she lost years going down the wrong track of thinking she was ugly (and that was the reason why boys were not keen on her) instead of realising that she was just in the wrong body. She said that she had never told anyone she hated her body because she did not think she would be taken seriously. She added that online or when playing through her male avatar – Jake – she felt finally at ease in her body.

I said that she was worried I was not taking her seriously.

She said she was seeing me only because her parents would not let her take hormones unless she saw me. She did not expect me to understand her. But she had to go through the motions.

I said that given she felt she had to see me we could at least make the most of the time we had together to understand what it felt like to be her and help her get through this difficult time in her life. Jane nodded. I then asked her to describe to me a bit more what she felt like when she was playing online as Jake as I sensed that she had come alive when she recalled her online life.

Jane relaxed visibly and told me that when she was online as Jake she felt free, as if she could now do and say things that in her real-life female body she could not. She said that she was like she imagined she should have always been. She placed particular emphasis on how she enjoyed the feeling of Jake running because 'his legs are strong and it looks like he can go wherever he likes'. She enjoyed the sensation of strength in her body and while on line she sometimes felt 'as if my actual body is more substantial'. Sometimes this feeling carried over after she signed off and that made her feel more like going out and being with others.

I observed that her male avatar, Jake, made her feel she was strong and could help her to get away from a place inside her body and mind where she felt very ill at ease and unhappy. I added that feeling 'substantial' seemed important to her and that she felt this way when she expressed herself and related to others though Jake.

Jane said she had always felt unhappy but had never understood why she felt so bad. When relating to others through Jake, or when she used her male persona on line, she told me that others had respect for her, took her seriously and related to her as a strong person that 'you would not mess around with'.

I said that being a boy seemed to make her feel more attractive and confident, safer from attacks by others – more substantial.

She said that she could now not even understand how she had managed to be so 'girlie' for so long.

I asked her what 'girlie' meant.

In her reply Jane gave a very caricatured picture of a 'princess' girl: someone into pretty prints, obsessed with make-up and boys, and no brain.

I observed that it sounded like a bit of a cardboard cut out Princess that had no substance.

Jane replied in an animated way: 'Exactly! That's what I was trapped inside. That's why it's so liberating to cut my hair, change my clothes and breathe!! Now I feel that I am someone. Well ... what I mean is that I'm me ...'

I said she seemed to have felt quite trapped but was she feeling trapped in the wrong sexed body or in an experience of herself that lacked substance ... someone who failed to make an impression on others?

Jane paused for a minute and then said that her father was very stuck in gendered roles and that her mother had been stuck in a 'hostess' role much of her life. Her mother was very invested in what other people thought, in the appearance of things, but actually Jane thought that her mother was the kind of person that did not make much of an impression on people: 'All those pretty dresses, all the lovely well-plumped-up cushions, but I'm not sure anyone really thinks she has a brain ... But this has nothing to do with what's happening to me', she added, 'I know I am trans, a boy, and that's what I need to follow.'

I commented that no sooner had she allowed us both to take an excursion away from the 'I am trans and I need to take hormones' track and to think more generally about what it felt like to be in her girl self and body, she had done a U-turn back into certainty about 'really being a boy'.

And so it was for several months: alternating between anger towards me for what she perceived to be my attempts to get her to think about something other than her wish to transition and brief moments when some other feelings and thoughts could be aired and explored.

During the first few months of our work I was especially struck by how Jane's experiences online appeared to open her up to her lived embodiment in a way that supported the work of the therapy. By actively encouraging her to tell me about her online activities and how Jake's physicality impacted on her mood and sense of herself online and offline, I began to think that her use of technology to experiment with her ideal self – her imagined embodiment – aided our analytic work. I was aware that it was only when I was able to approach her virtual life in my own mind as a process of 'becoming' in the sense I described earlier, and not as primarily defensive, that I was able to engage her in a dialogue with me about the meaning of her virtual world and virtual self.

The technical point here is that this conceptual stance supported an analytic stance that approached the relationship between her body and technology as a process that led to particular outcomes for her specifically and that could not be anticipated in any predetermined way. Moreover, this might not have been possible solely through verbal articulation of her experience in the context of the therapeutic process. Jane helped me to understand that Jake's virtual physicality literally gave her an embodied experience of her desire, fantasies and ghosts (I have in mind here the boy she should have been, for example, as I will shortly explain). This virtual body enabled her to explore in an affectively rich and experience-near manner what we could only put words to in our work.

An important breakthrough came a year into the therapy when Jane told me that in her biological mother's culture of origin boys were more highly prized and that she had sometimes wondered whether if she had been born a boy her mother might have kept her. This helped us to explore some of the fantasies about her adoption and how this related to her long-standing confusion about her iden-tity – her so-called 'substance' – that had become rigidly resolved by a retreat into certainty about being in the wrong body. As Jane explored and experimented with 'being a boy' within her online life (and to a lesser extent in her day-to-day life through her altered physical appearance), she was able to anchor herself in a body that felt more substantial. Importantly, it also allowed her all the associ-ated fantasies that, being a boy, she would have been wanted by her biological mother and that she would be noticed more generally and be taken seriously. This pointed to her ambivalent relationship with her adoptive mother who she felt failed to make an impression on others despite her focus on the body's surface appearance or the appearance of the 'body' of the house (the plumped-up cushions).

Two years on Jane has neither pursued hormone therapy nor construed what she needs to do in terms of transitioning. Let me be clear: I do not consider that there is a predetermined aim to therapy with transgendered individuals. However, in this particular case I did consider that Jane's label 'trans' was the only way she could begin to explore conflicts that had very little to do with her gender identity as such and that changing her body would not address her anxieties.

Jane continues to dress androgynously but in a way that nevertheless frames her feminine features and reveals how attractive she is. She started a relationship with a girl but it is clear that she is also drawn to boys. She spends less time online and now relates to others online as Jane. Her former male avatar is now a tall, strong woman who has breasts and athletic legs. Jane still struggles with what she perceives to be her actual small frame. Through her new female avatar's embodied form she expresses the need for a sturdy frame to give her the strong foundations and stability she feels she needs to be herself in the world. She has started to consider tracing her biological mother.

Mr B

Mr B was a professionally successful man in his forties who came to three-times-weekly analytic psychotherapy (face-to-face for the first two years) because of marital difficulties. He felt he was homosexual although he had not yet had any sexual relationships with men at that point.

Mr B had been married for five years when he started therapy and had one child. As a child Mr B had grown up in a religious, conservative family of high achievers. His mother was experienced as physically distant and brusque in her physical handling of him. Both parents had frowned upon sex outside marriage. Homosexuality was explicitly relegated to the category of 'perversions'.

Mr B recalled being tormented at secondary school by his attraction to an older boy. He masturbated to the fantasy of this boy and said that he invariably felt anxious once he had climaxed. He never had any sexual experiences with others until he went to university. His first sexual experiences comprised rather desultory encounters with women during which he often felt impotent. Again, as had happened at secondary school, he became fixated on a male university acquaintance, but never dared to actualise his strong homosexual desire.

He said that he had always hated his appearance. He thought his legs were too short and that his skin was too fair, 'like I blend into the background at best and at worst I look like a cadaver', he said. He had contemplated an eyebrow transplant because his eyebrows were so fair that it looked like he had shaved them off. I had taken up over time various dimensions of his experience of his body: how inhospitable his body felt to him, his deep-seated anxiety that his body betrayed how he felt: that he had nothing alive in him, that his skin and his hair were so light that they made him invisible to the other, and that he desperately wanted me to resuscitate something dead inside him.

Mr B did eventually make use of male prostitutes prior to fully coming out. Before taking this step, and that as I have discussed elsewhere could be construed in this instance as a developmental step towards integrating his sexuality (Lemma, 2015b), Mr B relied extensively on Internet pornography and gay chat rooms. This played a vital part in helping him to feel validated in his body and sexuality. I should add that he was not drawn to fetishistic or violent porn.

I will now very selectively focus on some dreams to illustrate the progressive elaboration of his representation of his sexual body via his use of cybersex and obviously also through the analytic process that ran concurrently with this. Due to time constraints I cannot provide detailed process reports.

At first when he accessed porn or when in gay chat rooms Mr B felt very inadequate and could not always reach orgasm. He was plagued by intrusive thoughts either about how unattractive he was or about his 'dirty' sexuality. He avoided visual contact online to begin with because he felt he was very unattractive. A dream from this early phase captures his denigrated bodily representation:

> *I am trapped in a dirty loo with my pants on the floor. There is shit everywhere on my legs. I have terrible diarrhoea and it floods the floor. The stench is overwhelming and I can hear people in the other cubicles wrenching, struggling to get out.*

When Mr B brought this dream I took it up in the transference as an expression of his terrible anxiety that his body and his homosexual desire would disgust me and that this would lead me to abandon him. He linked this to the disgust he felt his father had expressed towards gay men and that he realised he was fully identified with. We also looked at the dream (given some of his subsequent associations) as giving expression to his aggression and wish to cover me/his father with his shit in retaliation for the perceived rejection of his sexual self.

Nine months later, after regular, almost daily use of Internet gay chat rooms and largely text-based cybersex, he brought this dream:

> *I am in the gym. My leg muscles are taught. I have worked up a sweat and the man next to me looks at me intently. I am not sure if he's coming on to me or is repelled by my odour.*

In his associations Mr B told me that when he was in chat rooms he often felt 'confused' as he was not always sure if other men found him attractive, especially if the chat room involved visual contact. He felt safer using porn or just texting online because he was not being looked at. Within those boundaries he felt he could be in his own body more comfortably and express his sexual self with less inhibition.

We understood this second dream as expressing his difficulty in reading sexual signals when the interaction was visual and involved his actual body, even if once removed, and his ongoing anxiety about how to read my looking at him as he revealed to me more about himself: was I approving or still repelled by what he told me and what I saw. He was indeed at this stage still terrified about the possibility of revealing his homosexuality openly and could not even countenance 'actually' having sex with a man. However, although this second dream is still full of anxiety (and aggression towards the felt-to-be rejecting other: his odour is also a weapon with which to push away the other), I took it as a sign of the beginning of an elaboration of the possibility that the other might desire him: '*I am not sure if he's coming on to me ...*' I understood this to be a possibility that had been facilitated through the virtual exchanges in cyberspace as he imagined himself as potentially desirable and was altering his experience of embodiment.

During the following months in his therapy Mr B was very preoccupied with 'coming out' and I sensed that this was now something that he wanted to do and that had become more possible because of his experimentation online and the validation he had found there – as well as his analysis, I think. He started now to visit prostitutes and his use of Internet porn and chat rooms declined significantly. After one of the encounters with a prostitute he had sex with a few times and whose manner he liked, Mr B brought a very vivid dream:

> *He was a child and he was cooking but had no idea what ingredients he needed. He was looking for the cookery book his grandmother used but be could not find it. He decided to throw in the ingredients he had to hand and he started mixing a dough-like texture that looks golden and gradually thickens. His mother was shouting at him in the background calling him an idiot, that he should not even try to cook, that this was something only grown ups did.*

In his associations Mr B said that his mother was not at all like that in reality: she was 'mousy', a quiet woman. His grandmother by contrast was a strong character who had devoted herself to her work as a teacher at a girls' school and became a surrogate mother to several of the girls who still wrote to her in gratitude.

We understood this third dream as giving expression to his gratitude to the male prostitute for helping him to learn about himself sexually, that it was as if he had given him a book that contained the recipe for his sexuality, but that as soon as he knew what he needed, who he was, this then gave rise to a disapproving voice in his head that cut him down to size, telling him he was only a child who does not know what he is doing. I linked this to the way that no sooner had he told me how much he had enjoyed sex I had become this humiliating other who would cut him down to 'heterosexual child size'.

Mr B carried inside himself a feeling not only that his homosexuality was unacceptable, but also that simply 'being sexual' was shameful resulting in a pretend life that concealed his homosexual longings and that gave rise to a recurrent experience of me in the transference as disapproving and castrating.

Through virtual sexual encounters in cyberspace, as well as the use of porn and eventually the use of prostitutes, Mr B's dreams reveal the painful, but I am suggesting steady, changes in his representation of his body. After his actual encounter with a male prostitute he produces the third dream in which he cooks a 'dough-like texture that looks golden and gradually thickens', which reflected, as I understood it, his emergent representation of a sexual body that had colour/life and substance.

Of course a case like this begs the question of why Mr B could not work through his sexual conflicts primarily in the transference. I have some thoughts about this. Mr B recalled that both his parents were 'rigid' in everything they did, including how they presented themselves physically, which was a 'no frills' look as he described it. He had no memories at all of physical closeness with either parent. He experienced his body as 'dead' and this was reflected in his appearance, which was smart but 'grey'. His 'too fair' skin and his invisible eyebrows conjured up his representation of a body without contours that could so easily disappear into the background and die. Mr B therefore reported an early history characterised by what we could formulate as an undercathexis of the body by key attachment figures. In other words, he approached the development of his sexuality from a weak foundation at the level of his mental representation of his body. His struggle to integrate psychosexuality required analysis of this deficit, that is of his undercathected body self in the context of his earliest attachments, and an acceptance of the use he made of cyberspace to work through these difficulties rather than interpretation of it in the early stages.

Marked and contingent mirroring of the self's bodily experience is most likely, for us all, a vitally important feature of the development of a coherent sense of self firmly rooted in the body. Without such a foundation the trajectory to the satisfactory elaboration of the sexual self will most likely be compromised to varying degrees. My understanding was that Mr B's deficit at this level undermined his ability to symbolically represent his sexual desire, anxieties and conflicts. He had to first experience the sexual look and touch of the virtual sexual other, and then the actual touch and look of the prostitute, to enable him to feel safe but excitingly sexual in the context of an emotionally intimate relationship, which he went on to develop once he came out and left his wife a few years into the therapy.

In the transference I was conscious that Mr B anticipated my critical, non-desiring look and he avoided the couch at first so as to anxiously monitor it. I was conscious too of an absence of any erotic feelings in the transference as if his sexuality had to be kept away from our relationship.

The early deficit in Mr B's representation of his body could be said to have compromised the development of a phallic sexual self as a necessary step towards the integration of Oedipal sexuality. Perhaps one 'advantage' of the virtual sexual partner and later of the prostitute is precisely because they are not mother/father nor sexual partner nor analyst. The virtual sexual other and the prostitutes can thus support the development of a phallic sexual self bypassing Oedipal anxieties that cannot yet be faced. This allowed Mr B's body representation to become more consolidated in his mind before he could work through his Oedipal sexuality in the transference. This raises the possibility that such 'virtual sexuality' and then 'mirrored sexuality' – both of a narcissistic nature – are precursors of a 'relational sexuality' rooted in two bodies and minds that interact with each other and can then mirror each other reciprocally.

Mr B's individual trajectory suggests that it is important for the analyst to keep an open mind with respect to the use made of cyberspace to experiment with imagined embodiments. This may be especially relevant to the development of a consolidated sexual identity that can be subsequently lived out in the context of an attachment relationship.

At the start of his analysis Mr B was involved in what would technically be regarded by many as 'acting out'. The consolidation of the work of representation and its integrative potentialities made it possible, over time, for his sexuality to be explored in the transference/countertransference dynamic and to be elaborated psychically. This resulted in Mr B's capacity to make some important changes in his life congruent with who he felt himself to be and to eventually bear the depressive anxieties and guilt associated with his 'coming out' as homosexual. In my understanding of this analysis Mr B's use of cyberspace, and my approach to it as essentially 'progressive', highlights the potentially integrative value of a lateral transference. The latter concept is not much used in British and North American psychoanalysis but it is helpful for thinking about the need some patients have, as Denis (2011) puts it, for 'un espace de jeu lateral' when faced with the intensity of affects and fantasies mobilised in the transference. However, even when we allow the patient to use this 'space' without immediately interpreting it, the ultimate goal as far as I am concerned remains to eventually interpret *in* the transference, as was the case with Mr B.

Even if we consider Mr B's use of cyberspace to reflect a displacement of the intensity of the transference, through his online experiences, and which provided an opportunity to experience a progressively imagined embodiment, we might consider that Mr B had a 'new' embodied experience of himself that supported development *in the context of an analytic process* where the vicissitudes of this development (in all its regressive and progressive aspects) could eventually be reflected upon. In this particular case, and clearly not always, we could then say that the virtual space supported the work of analysis. To recognise it as such is important therapeutically and has implications for technique. It requires the therapist to sensitively steer a difficult path between helping the patient to represent experience and understanding and accepting for a time the teleological imperative that runs counter to that, which may nevertheless be a necessary step towards representing sexuality and living comfortably in the sexual body. Such a step may be aided by the use of cyberspace to experiment with one's experience of embodiment.

Somatic flexibility

Keeping in mind Jane's and Mr B's experiences I now want to think more generally about how the so-called freedom afforded by cyberspace for somatic flexibility might impact on an individual's body image and sense of self.

First we need to remember that cyberspace affords both visual and non-visual interaction, as I noted earlier. Some interactions in cyberspace suspend the force of the image, such as texting for example, that deploys mechanistic means for facilitating the performance of identity beyond the constraints imposed by physical appearance. The transformational potential of new media stems from how it allows us to suspend existing cultural figurations of the self (e.g. race, gender) (Poster, 2006). By decoupling identity from an analogical relation to the visible body online self-invention effectively places everyone in the position of having to mime his or her identity. Needless to say there are social and unconscious constraints that permeate virtual spaces: gender and class inevitably continue to structure the explicit possibilities for self-invention and dictate the ethos of online interaction. Virtual bodies are always necessarily embedded in pre-virtual material, social relations and internalised relationships and as such cannot but incorporate social practices that categorise and standardise bodies. Technology is not a-social or a-cultural; at some level it is inevitably always also political.

Second we need to be open to the possibility that virtual spaces might promote the development of an offline self by focusing on the enhancement of one's cyberself or body. If so then we need to consider whether individuals will seek parity with themselves across domains or will they be content simply to compartmentalise each identity (Suler, 2004) restricting it to the confines and context specificity of each 'on-' or 'off-'line world.

The identities that some individuals create for their characters online suggest that cyberspace is an environment in which they feel inclined to create characters imbued with their ideal selves. Béssiere *et al.* (2007) found that individuals who score lower on measures of psychological well-being are more likely to create characters who are closer to their ideal self and less like their actual self than those who score higher on measures of psychological well-being. Some of the interesting questions that arise from this finding concern the extent to which the possible selves that are realised in cyberspace are authentic expressions of one's self and, importantly, whether being authentic or not in these spaces is psychologically important. If through the process of virtual immediacy one can virtually realise the 'possible self' and in the process receive some form of social validation even if context-specific, then to what extent is this possible self 'authentic' and how might the way others react to this virtual self impact on the offline self?

Here it becomes critical to keep in mind the distinction between an *ideal realisation* of embodiment from an *idealised realisation*, which would be equated with inauthentic embodiment. For certain individuals their avatar has the potential to create a large discrepancy between their perceived identity status in the 'real' world and that obtainable in cyberspace. How one experiences oneself will therefore change.

Large discrepancies between the offline body image and one's avatar may lead some individuals to favour or even fixate on their avatar self resulting in the psychic dominance of the virtual over the non-virtual, which in turn may result in individuals spending more and more time in a state where their sense of self is perceived to be enhanced. The risk here is that the individual can inhabit what Law (2013) has termed an 'atomocracy', that is a personal world of one. Law is writing outside of a psychoanalytic frame but his term aptly captures a narcissistic state characterised by complete omnipotence where the laws of the reality principle no longer apply.

Concluding thoughts

We are born a body and we have to become one. The body is more than a modality for expressing the self or identity: it is where I exist (Milon, 2005). The body is always in a process of becoming, embodying sameness and difference, forever adjusting and unfinished. Encapsulated in the French notion of *entredeux* ('between two'), the body is temporal and dynamic, representing the middle. As Deleuze urged us to do, we need to think in terms of 'lines' rather than 'points':

> It is never the beginning or the end which are interesting; the beginning and end are points. What is interesting is the middle. (Deleuze and Parnet, 2002: 39)

In our thinking and clinical practice we need attend to the complex ways in which bodies and technology are entwined. By conceiving of bodies and technology in a 'constitutive relationality' (Coleman, 2011) a psycho-analytic approach to the relations between them can easily go beyond an account of the 'negative effects' of technology. This approach invites us to explore how bodies continue to become through their relations with technology. A clinician does not need to understand what technology is but how it interacts with the patient's subjective experience of the body.

We each have a corporeal history: both ontological and phylogenetic. When we approach the lived body we are obliged to take into account the way the experiential body is constituted through multiple worlds of the imagination, of the artificial, of the simulated and of the real world. New technologies and media cannot be simply conceived of as 'tools', as means to an end goal in the service of pre-given bodies. Instead they have created a new environment that brings about new corporealities corre-sponding to space worlds and time worlds that have not existed before (Holmes, 1997). Our daily analytic practice unfolds in this environment – for better and for worse.

The techno environments of cyberspace are particularly receptive to the projection and acting out of unconscious fantasy – such as we can observe in the compulsive use of Internet porn as Wood (2014) has focused on in her work – and like all 'good' things they may be put to less good use. If we conceive of the virtual as simply one more realm among others that can be accessed through embodied perception or emotion these 'new' spaces can function as yet another theatre for the unfolding of the internal world and thereby may provide, in some cases, helpful bridges to the work of representation in the context of an analytic process. This highlights the potentially integrative value of what we could regard as 'lateral transfer-ence'. The latter concept is not much used in British and North American psychoanalysis but it is helpful for thinking about the need some patients have, as Denis (2011) puts it, for 'un éspace de jeu lateral' when faced with the intensity of affects and fantasies mobilised in the transference, allowing the patient to use this 'space' without immediately interpreting it.

We therefore need to consider the contingent relations that exist between a given space and what that space affords in terms of representa-tion and interaction and how this feeds into the development of identity. And as we do so we need to keep firmly in mind that what transcends the online and offline spaces is the individual. In thinking about the world of cyberspace, we need to consider not whether technology is good or bad, but whether psychologically the individual can cope with what is being presented or enacted within a given virtual space. This is why generalities are of limited value. This is why we need a psychoanalytic lens to focus on how technology interacts for better or for worse with particular psychic economies.

Notes

1   In referring to cyberspace I am drawing on Stratton's definition (1997: 29): 'the space produced by human communication when it is mediated by technology in such a way that the body is absent'.
2   This is an important point because as smartphones and computers have become as common as the car but are now more essential than the car has ever been to everyday life, digital natives will relate to these objects qualitatively differently on a bodily level compared to digital immigrants. It will, of course, not be long before we will also cease to talk about digital natives and immigrants as there will only be the natives ...
3   Central to Deleuze's notion of becoming is that subjects and objects are replaced with 'bodies'. In a Deleuzian sense, bodies refer not necessarily to human bodies but to multiple and diverse series of connections which assemble to form a particular spatial and temporal moment (Deleuze and Guattari, 1987). Multiplicity and difference are key to Deleuze's concept of becoming and it is through the connections between multiple and different things that bodies must be understood.
4   Together with 'difference', 'becoming' is an important component of Deleuze's corpus. In so far as Deleuze champions a particular ontology, these two concepts are its cornerstones.
5   'Becoming has neither beginning nor end, departure or arrival, origin nor destination ... a line of becoming has only a middle' (Deleuze and Guatarri, 1987: 231).

Chapter 2

The black mirror

Becoming sexual in the digital age

Through the staggering advances in technology (and I am using the term here in its broadest sense to encompass medical and cybernetic technologies) we can now manipulate our bodies in actuality and virtually and hence our so-called identity. There is also unprecedented access to sexual images wherever one is, whenever one wants. It is possible to engage sexually with others without sharing the same physical space with them, setting a new context for the development of sexual identity in particular. I will restrict myself in this chapter to addressing the impact of technology, and especially of life in cyber-space, on the development of sexual identity during adolescence. This is not only because so much of my clinical experience has been with this age group but also because nowhere is the struggle for identity, for defining this 'I', more urgent, more poignant and all too often more desperate than during adolescence.

While much of the early Internet hype forecast that new online tech-nologies would suddenly allow us to cast off the shackles of hegemonic gender, race, class or sexuality and redefine ourselves in any way imagi-nable, I want to suggest that this is not the case. Cyberspace is far from a utopian site of identity fluidity and play. The Internet as a 'queer' space with the potential for negotiating and performing one's identity has not delivered its promise despite seducing many along the way. Instead of casting off these shackles and becoming free-floating entities in cyber-space, the body and its unconscious identifications as they manifest in our conscious relationship to our sexuality remains a psychically organising principle even when the body is effectively disintermediated in cyber-space. Virtual bodies are always necessarily embedded in pre-virtual internal and external material relationships.

Definitions

Before going any further let me define first, and all too schematically, what I mean by sexual identity. This is not an easy task since the concept of identity itself has no place in metapsychology. Of all the disciplines concerned with defining 'selfhood' or 'identity' psychoanalysis is the boldest by introducing the subversive machinations of the unconscious and the 'speciousness' of identity itself (Frosh, 1991). Identity, while consciously experienced as defining the core parameters of who we feel ourselves to be, is always forged through unconscious processes of projection and introjection. It provides an illusion of continuity, which is adaptive to varying degrees.

To understand sexual identity we must return first to Freud (1923c) and his understanding that the ego is 'first and foremost a body-ego; it is not merely a surface entity but it is itself the projection of a surface' (1923c: 26), that is the most primitive form of self-representation is a body representation. For Freud the ego was thus represented as a psychical map, a projection of the surface of the body. More specifically, the ego was seen to be a mental representation of the individual's perceived libidinised relationship to his body.

Freud (1923c) – and later Schilder (1950) in his landmark study of the body image – both essentially underline how at the beginning of life internal perceptions are more fundamental than external ones in shaping the ego. In other words throughout life ego structure and identity are founded to a significant degree on the sensations and awareness of the body (Hägglund and Piha, 1980). Aulagnier (1975) underscores how the baby's somatic experience (*le vecu somatique*) 'anticipates an I', as she puts it, even prior to the baby's encounter with otherness. Freud thus cemented the view, later developed by others, that the body-ego is the container and foundation for the sense of self[1] (Mahler and Furer, 1968; Winnicott, 1966, 1972; Haag, 1985; Krueger, 1989; Sandler,1994).

So far I am suggesting that we cannot think about identity without thinking about the body. And we cannot think about the body without considering sexuality. The body is crucial to understanding a person's experience of their identity and one of its most important aspects is its manifestation and apprehension of sexuality: sexuality is an integral part of life, a consequence of embodiment. As Baudrillard suggests, 'Sex is not a function, it is what makes a body a body' (1994: 98).

There is no agreement among analysts as to what constitutes sexual identity and whether it differs from gender identity (Birksted-Breen,

2016) and these debates are beyond the scope of this chapter. Generally speaking, however, gender identity is not considered to be causally related to sexual desire and both are typically conceptualised as independent of sexed bodies. It is clear that sexuality has an immensely generative power that refuses to be distributed along familiar lines of heteronormative procreation and normative gender roles. For me the strength of an analytic account of sexuality is that it reveals that the relationship between a body part and its sexual function is at best one of lightly tethered consonance rather than a rigidly shackled indexical mapping. We all have psychic investments in our bodies. We cannot isolate the materiality of the body from the messy tangles of inscription and meaning that arise from internal as well as external forces. Severed from its psychic investments the materiality of the body has no meaning. It is only Real in the Lacanian sense of the word, foreclosed from language, symbolisation and meaning.

The sexed body, social gender and sexuality (i.e. desire) – distinctions first elaborated by the early twentieth-century sexologists – are all constitutive of sexual identity. For the purposes of this chapter, suffice it to say that I define 'sexual identity' as the superordinate category of which the following are the component parts comprising the central aspects shaping one's subjective of 'myself as sexual': the object of desire, gender identifications, conscious and unconscious aspects of sexual fantasies and body image. Sexual identity, as I understand it, thus reflects the outcome – the psychic compromise – of the individual's attempts at integration of infantile sexuality (Laplanche's (2011) 'le sexual') and pubertal sexuality. As Laufer and Laufer (1984) suggest it is only during adolescence that the content of the sexual wishes and the Oedipal identifications become integrated into an irreversible sexual identity.

From latency to blatancy

Having now set out some definitional parameters let us get back to Freud's conceptualisation of sexual development as the basis from which to reflect on the impact of new technologies/media on the development of sexual identity.

Freud emphasised that the child's sexual fantasies are intense and experienced as powerfully exciting and potentially frightening. He detailed the long, erotically stimulating, sensual period of infancy and childhood in which the child absorbs and contains endless sensual moments of physical contact, without the cognitive resources to make sense of these experiences.

Then followed an 'incubation period' – the so-called latency stage – a cooling down period for drive-related activities (Freud, 1930) prefacing the upheaval of puberty.

However, when we consider sexual development in the digital age we need to consider the validity of the notion of a latency stage. We are now seeing children who are at the latency stage but seem to be less and less 'latent'. Instead of latency there is what I call *blatancy*: the latency age child remains as excitable as the Oedipal child and 'infantile modes of sexuality remain continuously manifest from the oedipal stage onwards characterised by an unrestrained arousal of infantile genitality' (Guignard, 2014: 65).

Because of the ready availability of Internet pornography, even the very young are now exposed to imagery they would once have had to work hard to seek out and that some stumble across unintentionally. Playground discussions about sex are more detailed and advanced reflecting exposure to sexual imagery that would simply not have been available to children and young people pre-Internet. Some of the YouTube pornography videos that reliably 'do the rounds' in the playgrounds of primary school-age children involve hardcore, fetishistic sex that would be disturbing to many adults.

Along with several analysts (e.g. Guignard, 2014) I no longer think that it makes sense to conceptualise sexual development with respect to a latency stage. However, I consider that sexual development takes on a specific transformation with the advent of puberty and that this represents a point of crisis for many adolescents. The period of adolescence has indeed been described by several authors as involving an identity crisis (Blos, 1967; Erikson, 1968; Briggs, 2002), but this requires some qualification: the psychic process of adolescence typically sets in motion an unsettling review of personal identity that is *rooted in the body*. One of the most important challenges to articulating identity during adolescence is that the young person has to integrate their changing pubertal body into the image they have of themselves. At the best of times puberty thus initiates a complicated and unsettling internal process.

The delicate and intricate processes that support the establishment of a secure sense of self confidently rooted in the body, and the capacity to reflect on experience rather than enact it on and through the body, may be further undermined by the relentless emphasis on transformation, change and triumph over the body now made possible by new technologies. These external trends do not cause new forms of psychopathology per se, but rather they may have an adverse impact on the young person's capacity to integrate the reality of the sexual body into the self-representation. Some young people will be more vulnerable to this than others (Lemma, 2011).

In their detailed work on adolescence, Laufer and Laufer (1984) have highlighted the need to change one's relationship to the body as the key task of adolescent development. Its outcome, they suggest, determines the final sexual identity on which the sense of self is based. The demands made by this developmental transition, however, can be for some young people simply too much to bear (Laufer and Laufer, 1984; Bronstein, 2009; Flanders, 2009), even 'catastrophic' (Bion, 1970). Meltzer (1967) refers to the 'confusional anxiety' that he regards as typical for adolescents. This is all the more so where the quality of early relationships has contributed to a fragile, undercathected bodily self, or to entrenched splitting such that body parts may have become identified with bad, terrifying objects. In such cases an internal or external organ can be experienced as an alien object residing within the body rather than as an integrated part of the body self. Body sensations may then need to be kept separate from the image of oneself as sexually mature.

The black mirror: The adolescent's 'second look'

Any consideration of the development of the body self, and hence of how the pubertal body is likely to be managed by the young person, as it were, requires us to consider the role of the earliest mirror. Throughout life mirrors – actual and symbolic – remain important. The Lacanian baby looks to the mirror to bring coherence to his fragmented embodied experience. The Winnicottian baby turns to the other-as-mirror, we might say, in order for his embodied experience to be mentalised. Irrespective of whether we understand this mirror in Lacanian or Winnicottian terms the search is for a reflection that is restitutive of a coherent, boundaried 'I' rooted in the body. Indeed, marked and contingent mirroring of the self's bodily experience is most likely to be, for us all, a vitally important feature of the development of a coherent sense of self firmly rooted in the body (Lemma, 2014).

If good-enough mothering can be said to depend on the mother's capacity to mirror back the child's experience, several authors have suggested that even the good enough mother reliably shows a marked failure of mirroring in one respect: that of the child's sexuality (Fonagy, 2008; Target, 2015). Sexuality stands alone in that it is the only intense, emotionally charged experience that the mother does not attempt to make sense of for the child. Yet such early arousal experiences become incorporated into elaborate systems of early sexual fantasy. To varying degrees early erotic fantasies are formed in response to experiences of a degree of overstimulation and shame and thus often inhibited, if not altogether repressed, and sometimes manifest in symptoms.

How does a child (and later the adolescent) make sense of their sexual urges and the fantasies that become organised around these early arousal experiences? Due to the 'appropriate' early parental mirroring failure when it comes to sexuality, we have here, I want to suggest, the seeds of a split at the very core of the experience of embodiment: some aspects of our embodied experience are accurately mirrored, but not so when the body is perceived by the other as the site for the infant's nascent sexual self. This inscribes a sense of incongruence at the heart of psychosexuality, of a 'misreading' in relation to the experience of the self (Fonagy, 2008; Stein, 1998a, 1998b; Target, 2015). Importantly, however, I want to underline that this incongruence structures the child's *embodied* experience such that the body image, even when all goes well in early development, is predicated on a split between the sexual and non-sexual body, which forcefully presses for integration at puberty. When this fails we can observe developmental breakdown typically expressed in the language of the body.

But where, or to whom, does the adolescent turn to transform this so-called incongruence into something that can be mentally represented in order to then integrate the sexual and non-sexual body into a coherent representation of the body in the mind? I want to suggest that at puberty the adolescent needs a mirror to take a 'second look' at a body whose pre-pubescent integrity is shattered by the genital uprising. This recasts the young person in the original position of the infant whose subjective experience of his body 'in bits-and-pieces' (Lacan, 1977) pushed the then infant to look into the mirror for the integration that the infant's mind could yet perform for itself. At puberty, however, the body is an explicitly sexual one for all to see: even harder to ignore but still difficult to mirror its now poignant, now unruly and for some parents now disturbing, undeniable sexuality. Just as the mother of infancy turns away from reflecting back the baby's sexuality, parents appropriately turn away a second time round at puberty, even of this turning away, in the best of circumstances, is more nuanced. Some parents manage to strike a helpful balance between providing some validation of the young person's sexuality and an appropriate 'turning away' from it.

But all adolescents are propelled to look for a mirror beyond the parental figures to elaborate and consolidate a sexual identity. Pre-Internet this mirror was primarily provided by peers and media such as TV, cinema, music, books and top-shelf pornography magazines. The most readily available and deployed mirror in the twenty-first century that has supplanted all others is the *black mirror*. This is the one you will find on virtually every desk, in every home and in the palm of every hand: the cold, shiny screen of a monitor, tablet or phone.

Mobile and online technologies have brought enormous opportunities for pleasure and communication, knowledge-seeking and exchange. The Internet, like earlier print pornography and shared experiences among peers regarding masturbation, facilitates the normalisation of adolescents' sexual feelings (Shapiro, 2008; Galatzer-Levy, 2012). But these new technologies also bring as yet unexamined risks for young people. In order to understand the nature of the risks we have to understand the nature of this so-called 'mirror'.

The black mirror not only differs from previous media in terms of the unprecedented range of the sexual content it screens, but also in the very distinctive way that it operates. This mirror does not reflect back; rather it intrusively projects into the viewer. It 'pushes' (think, for example, of the 'push notification' function on your smartphones) desires, images and sensations into the body and mind even when the young person has not asked for them. Instead, as the young person looks at the computer screen, an orgy of possibility hits him: a sexuality à la carte is served up with myriad configurations of bodies (e.g. men with fully grown breasts *and* a penis). The Internet fosters a childlike state of sexual curiosity (Wood, 2011), an 'open all hours' sexual policy where the parental bedroom is never shut and the primal scene can be watched over and over from the safety of the child's bedroom.

A further important implication for the articulation of sexual identity is the fact that Internet pornography can now be accessed easily and rapidly, that is the black mirror facilitates *immediacy without mediation*. There is no tension, no conflict, no waiting with respect to the satisfaction of sexual desire whatever its psychic function. Without exposure to the experience of delay or frustration desire loses its 3D shape (see Chapter 3) that would allow for the various dimensions of the experience of desire to be represented in the mind. The combination of immediacy without mediation and the 'blatancy' of online pornographic images leave no room for the stillness and slowness that makes the work of representation necessary and possible. Instead a kind of *scoping looting* is encouraged online: hundreds of sexual images intoxicate the mind, inviting a 'smash and grab' approach to sexual fantasy and desire. Importantly the images/fantasies that are seized in this manner are ultimately not felt to be one's own (Galatzer-Levy, 2012).

The black mirror can seduce the young person struggling to make sense of their disruptive sexual body by supplying concrete images and sexual scenarios that provide a close technicolour match to the central masturbation fantasy (Laufer, 1976), now socially sanctioned through the medium of technology. This, in turn, offers some validation for something that feels disturbing within, but since the black mirror supplies the ready made sexual scenarios these need not be owned as belonging to the self thereby undermining the establishment of an integrated sexual identity. I hope to now illustrate some of these themes through my work with Celina.

Celina

Celina was a few months away from her seventeenth birthday when she first came to see me. A once-weekly arrangement soon increased to three-times-weekly sessions on the couch.

Celina was one of two children. Her father committed suicide when Celina was about seven. He was suffering from bipolar disorder. Her mother eventually remarried when Celina was 14 at which point Celina's state of mind became a worry to her mother. She felt that Celina, who up until then had seemingly been functioning relatively well, all things considered, became withdrawn, spending long periods of time shut off in her room on the Internet. She lost interest in her studies, which she was very good at, and although she sometimes went out with friends her mother felt that she was only superficially connected with her peer group.

The trigger for seeking help was the discovery by her stepfather that Celina was downloading hardcore pornography on her computer. The parents had been deeply disturbed by its content, which pointed to Celina's fascination with sado-masochistic practices. It later transpired in our work that Celina was devoting on average four hours per day on the Internet after school (more at weekends) and much of this time was spent looking at pornography and frequently masturbating to this.

Celina was angry with her stepfather for 'grassing on me' and yet I detected some relief that she had been found out as she was herself very worried that, like her own father, she was losing her mind and would end up with no option but to kill herself. She had expressed suicidal ideation after she was found out.

She did not have any emotionally intimate relationships with either boys or girls, but she had been sexually active with both boys and girls albeit in a rather limited fashion. Upon meeting me the first time Celina announced that she was 'trans' and insisted rather forcefully that 'I know who I am' and did not need help with her sexuality. When I asked her about why she was being so insistent about her sexuality given that I had not questioned it, Celina replied that her parents thought it was 'perverse' to fancy girls and boys and to look more masculine, as she did, and she was sure that I would think so too. She reassured me that many of her friends were 'bi' or 'trans', that times had moved on since her mother, or I, had been a teenager. She felt that her mother in particular was 'repulsed' by her sexuality.

The only thing that worried her was that she could not focus at school any longer. She admitted to downloading pornography in the past but refused for some time to discuss this with me saying that she had stopped doing this. However, several months into the therapy, in the sessions I will now share, she eventually told me, feeling very ashamed, that she had continued to access Internet pornography.

I will now draw on two brief excerpts from two consecutive sessions taken from the seventh month of our work together to illustrate, first, the compelling nature of the black mirror for Celina and second, how the Internet pornography that she masturbated to interfered with the elaboration of her own involvement in the perverse fantasy that was gripping her and thus prevented the establishment of a stable sexual identity.

Celina arrived 35 minutes late for her first session of the week. She was often late. Over time we understood the fantasy behind the lateness that was exciting to her: I was kept waiting, like her 'slave' was in the sexual fantasy she masturbated to, not knowing if she would come or if she was still alive. She was entirely in control. If I interpreted this I punctured the fantasy because then I was no longer enslaved to my worry and longing for her, which was defensively sexualised in her erotic scenario. I then had a mind of my own that she could not script. But her lateness, though embedded in this early sexualised transference dynamic, had taken a turn for the worse for a few weeks prior to the sessions here reported as she was feeling increasingly desperate about her anticipated exam failure and became very disorganised around all her commitments.

Celina lay on the couch and rather threateningly sighed and said:

Don't say anything. I *know* I am late. (Her tone was very prescriptive and domineering.)

This was followed by a long silence that she eventually broke.

I hate coming here. It's a waste of my time. If my mother's really worried about me her money would be better invested in getting me some tutors because I'm going to fail my exams. I don't understand ANYTHING about maths and I have exams soon. I just can't get my head round what any of it means ... I don't care about it ... Who fucking cares about numbers! Like that's going to change the world! (She said this with evident excitement and triumph.)

I said that arriving late was a way of making me long to see her walk through that door and be relieved that she was still alive. (This was a shared understanding between us by this stage.) But when she turned the analysis into her favoured sexual script, as she had done again today by arriving so late, it did turn it into 'wasted time'. And yet she was also letting me know that she felt increasingly out of control of her own mind and hopeless about the possibility of change.

Celina said that she didn't care about what I thought or about anything really. Her characteristic 'rant' continued but as she spoke her pace gradually slowed. The mania that normally punctuated her speech delivery gave way to more fragmented speech, starting and stopping sentences as if in the absence of rage, of mania, of sexual intoxication, she was inexorably dragged to a place in her mind where her thoughts fragmented and she was utterly hopeless. She did, however, manage one final expletive about how 'I have now wasted today's fucking session and you're bound to call time now.'

I observed that today she had not managed to entirely persuade herself or me that she did not care, that she was actually quite worried about her state of mind and worried about how she was depriving herself of my help by arriving late.

The next day she arrived 'only' 15 minutes late. She was restless on the couch, pulling her legs up to her chest as if she wanted to roll up into a ball, to cover her body and conceal it from my gaze.

I simply observed that today she was feeling anxious, maybe about what I might see.

The silence that ensued was very tense as she writhed on the couch. She eventually said that she was glad that she did not have to look at me, that I must think her repulsive and she wished analysis involved me lying on another couch, at the other end, coterminous with hers, where my head would be head-to-head with hers, so that neither she nor I could look at each other.

I said that this couch arrangement would mean that I could not look at her, but I would still be very close to her, that our two heads/minds could be close, as she revealed to me something that felt shameful and disturbing inside her mind.

The homosexual transference is in evidence here, but in this particular moment this did not feel as pressing as responding to both the activation of shame (the wish to not be seen) and Celina's need to feel that I could still bear to be close to her. This is why I decided to not interpret the transference more directly, but took up her barely disguised wish for closeness and acceptance at the point when she felt so ashamed.

She said yes, that she needed me to know something but she did not want me to look at her.

I asked her what she feared I might see.

She said that I would be disappointed and disgusted. She hated looking into my eyes when she walked into the room at the start of sessions and she wished she could also stop me from looking at her. She added that she hated her body because she looked disgusting. She hated the way her skin looked.

I said that perhaps she did not want either of us to look at something inside her that disgusted her, that was now experienced by her as being written all over her skin, but that this was something that also worried her and that she rather urgently needed my help with it.

Celina went very quiet. After five minutes she said very tentatively and anxiously: 'I've been lying to you ... I never stopped looking at porn ... I just do it in the early hours of the morning now, when I can be sure that my parents are asleep, and then I now make sure I delete all the browsing history as I'm sure my stepdad checks on me ...

Then she fell silent again. I sensed that she needed my help to tell me more, that if I stayed too silent instead of offering her a helpful space for reflection I would become the mother who is repulsed and who wants to look away and that this would close her down. I considered that given the acuteness of her anxiety she might not able to make use of an interpretation that addressed the object I had become.

... So I only said that she wanted me to know something more ... more than that she had never stopped downloading pornography ...

After some more silence, during which she kept moving restlessly on the couch, Celina then told me that whereas before she would climax four or five times per night and this would send her to sleep, she was worried that she now found it harder to orgasm to pornography. She sometimes rubbed herself very hard and 'tugged' at her clitoris for so long that she was in pain ... sometimes she enjoyed this pain and wished she could 'tear off' her clitoris ... This relieved her despite the pain, made her feel like nothing mattered in that moment ... She said rather anxiously that the sexual images she found exciting on the Internet were ones that she would never come up with herself: 'They're not in my head until I see them and then I keep going back to them. They're like wallpaper and then I get bored of it and re-paper the wall ... but now I have to keep changing the wallpaper.'

After another pause she added that the difficulty in climaxing had made her search for more disturbing images and videos on the Internet. She said: 'I cannot stop and ... sometimes ... I wish I could go somewhere, like men go to see a prostitute, and pay someone to do these things to me. One of my friends at school – he's the year above me – and he went to Soho and paid for sex.' She gave me a lot of detail about her friend's experience and her speech quickened. I sensed her state of mind changing. I could feel that she was both anxious and starting to get excited as she was psychically on her way to Soho in the session, as if she had shown me too much and she now had to recover some sexual musculature to manage her shame and anxiety.

By this time we were near the end of the session. I said she had managed to allow me to see her, she had opened her mind to me and showed me the wallpaper, and that she needed my help to *not* go to Soho and instead stay in the session with me. But I observed that there was also now an increasing pressure building between us as the session was coming to an end and Soho started to look more enticing – a place she could go to where she could pay someone other than me to take her pain away.

Celina burst out that she thought she was losing her mind: 'These images … they're not mine … do you understand? THIS IS NOT ME!!'

I said that part of the lure of the Internet pornography was that it temporarily allowed her to shut down the part of her mind that felt so confused, so full of anxiety and shame. But she was right: the more she tried to manage that in herself by looking at pornography, the more she was actually in danger of losing her mind, of not knowing what fantasies belonged to her, whether she could contain them, and most of all she was in danger of not knowing who she was.

Celina was quiet but when she resumed talking her tone struck me as more detached and contemptuous again: 'I guess you must be pleased now that you have got this out of me. I guess that's what you're paid to do … to extract the truth.'

I felt as if she had allowed me to see too much, that she had exposed her terrifying experience of not knowing who she was, and she then converted her anxiety and shame into her arousing sexual scenario, which afforded her a measure of control: I had now become the dominatrix who had painfully extracted the shameful truth and was now about to also call an end to the session. Celina was turning her pain into pleasure.

I eventually said that she had allowed me to know something today that was very disturbing to her, but now that I was about to call time, that she felt I was the one in control shutting her out until Thursday (the last session of the week for her). I had become harsh, a kind of torturer who extracted her thoughts and feelings without any real care but that this now did not cause her pain because we were in that familiar script that anesthetised her from feeling pain.

Celina ended the session in silence.

Discussion

There are many rich threads that could be elaborated on in this material but I will restrict myself to only three strands of thought directly pertinent to the black mirror and to the development of sexual identity during adolescence, namely:

1 some specific reflections on my work with Celina;
2 some general reflections about the function of masturbation and of pornography during adolescence; and finally
3 some thoughts about transgender identity.

1. From 'I know who I am' to 'This is NOT me'

Celina began her analytic journey stating with insistent certainty: 'I know who I am', she said to me as she declared herself 'trans'. The emotional truth that this statement of identity contained, as I understood it, was not one about her sexual identity, but about her desperate need to find an identity label to lend some coherence to her very disturbing sexual body, its unconscious identifications and the fantasies that she was compelled by. I will return to the point later.

Internet pornography became Celina's retreat. Perhaps the most visceral manifestation of her urgent need to find temporary coherence through sexual arousal and pain was the insistent 'tugging' at her clitoris, which she fantasised tearing off. Her choice of the word 'tugging', which we might think to be more commonly associated with how one handles a penis, conveys the confused relationship in her mind to her actual female genitalia that had become a combined 'clitoris-penis' at the level of her body representation with all the attendant unconscious meanings it held for her.

By the time we reached the sessions reported here Celina had travelled to a very difficult, uncertain place where she implored: 'This is *NOT* me'. She was now not sure who she was. She felt unmoored in her body and mind and hence without any stable identity. She wanted to distance herself from her sexual fantasies and disown them: they emanated from the black mirror and had no connection to her mind. Her plea is deeply evocative of one of the features of the black mirror that I outlined earlier, namely how it rapidly 'pushes' content into the mind cutting out the psychic work necessary for integrating meaning and assuming ownership of one's own mind. It also provides an all too easy way of divorcing oneself from one's own sexual fantasies: 'This is NOT me'.

The work by the Laufers has drawn attention to how, during adolescence, Oedipal wishes are experienced within the context of the young person having physically mature genitals and a compromise solution is found between what is wished for and what can be allowed. This compromise solution defines the person's sexual identity. The sexual fantasies that become the most compelling typically contain the various regressive satisfactions and the main sexual identifications and this is clear in Celina's case. Given the traumatic loss of her father, and what I eventually understood to have been her mother's long-standing depression that preceded the father's suicide and intensified following it, Celina was primed for a difficult adolescence as her body became the active force in sexual and aggressive fantasy and behaviour. Her defensive organisation, however, came under extreme stress at age 14 (she had started menstruating late in fact, only before her thirteenth birthday), around the time of the mother's remarriage. The retreat into Internet pornography escalated soon thereafter.

Celina's most compelling masturbatory fantasy followed a very clear script. The essential elements were that mostly, but not exclusively, the woman was the dominant partner while the men were invariably submissive, kept waiting for her attention. They would eventually be humiliated by being made to clean up different kinds of messes on the floor. As we came to understand it over time the fantasy reflected an alternating identification with both the castrated father who lost control of his mind and body and killed himself in what she fantasised to have been humiliating circumstances (i.e. 'the slave'), and her identification with the dominant, controlling, manic part of him that had been very exciting for her as a little girl (i.e. 'the dominatrix'). For example, she recalled how he would override what her mother said, effectively triumphing over her, such as taking away Celina for exciting escapades without letting the mother know their whereabouts.

Over time we understood her sexual fantasies as defending against catastrophic breakdown if she allowed herself to mourn the traumatic loss of her father, that is if she allowed herself to face the contents of her inner world. Instead the black mirror provided an alternative to looking inside. External images and scripted sexual scenarios covered up the all too painful and disturbing internal scenarios, supplying the sexual stimulation that turned the fear and grief she could not yet process into sexual excitement. Despite the phantasy that pain can be done away with, however, such a defensive strategy is costly to the self because the dead and living are now fused in concrete identification dominated by hatred (Freud, 1917; Lemma and Levy, 2004).

Celina not only had to manage the loss of her father but also the emotional fall-out that ensued when her mother remarried. Following the father's suicide and up until her mother's remarriage Celina had enjoyed a much closer relationship with her. She viewed her mother as kind but weak but after she met the stepfather she had become very angry with her and accused her of her being very 'conservative and dull'. It seemed that her mother's renewed sexuality when she met the stepfather had been experienced as threatening to Celina who felt shut out, on her own and very small again in the face of the new parental couple. The stepfather, in external reality, was a very important figure introducing much needed dilution of the intensity of the mother–daughter dyad, but he was also experienced as an intruder whom she wished to dominate and punish.

The dominatrix figure of Celina's sexual fantasies was a very tough, physically imposing woman with very well developed muscles: a figure with small breasts who looked very masculine. The fantasy accompanying masturbation seemed therefore to reflect an identification of Celina's body with that of her father as a further defensive measure against the hatred she felt towards her mother. This figure, as we came to understand it, expressed Celina's wish to triumph over her mother – she was now the phallic woman who could rescue at will the father from his castration and death and punish the stepfather for putting her back in her Oedipal place, as it were.

The Laufers suggest that the young person's defensive organisation is tested at puberty. The challenge for the adolescent is twofold: she needs to work out which parts of the content of the sexual fantasy, and which regressive wishes in general, are acceptable and which ones have to be repudiated; and at this pressure point she is also confronted 'with the adequacy or inadequacy of the defensive organization to help him deal with these problems' (Laufer and Laufer, 1984: 74). She may now feel that she has little ability to defend against certain regressive pulls. This is the point of greatest risk for some young people looking into the black mirror since one of the qualities of the Internet is that it appears to represent a seductive if 'corrupt superego', or to invite a dissolution of the superego, as Wood has suggested (2011, 2014). The black mirror removes all external obstacles: nothing has to be overcome in order to access pornography. Moreover, the speed of access to pornography diminishes the self's implication in the desire to look for sexual images.

Initially it appeared as if cyber-pornography would be no different from the old variety, the screen merely replacing the pornography magazine. The latter required not only physical stature in order to reach the 'top shelf', but also the overcoming of a degree of embarrassment or shame in order to physically make it to the newsagent, hold the magazine in one's hand, pay for it and then have to find physical places in which to hide it away, usually but not only from parental figures. The embodied experience of accessing pornography looked and felt very different pre-Internet. By removing all external obstacles to pornography the black mirror exposes the young person to a greater risk in the face of the regressive pull leading to a retreat away from genitality.

2. Examining dystopian myths: Do online and mobile technologies adversely impact on the sexual behaviour of young people?

In 2013 Porn Hub was the thirty-fifth most visited website for children aged 6–14 in the UK (Ofcom, 2013). If this rings alarm bells it is important to note that the survey covers a broad age span and we do not know how many of the younger children access these sites. Having said this it is clear that images that are now commonplace were once visible only to those who were determined to seek them out, knew where to go and were not ashamed to reveal their appetite for them. Now they can be reached at a click, without fear of disclosure or embarrassment. There is now not only quick access to pornography, but the way time itself is experienced when engaging with it is of note: time tends to be markedly foreshortened in pornography and the normalised image of sexual interaction becomes one in which there is a hurried movement from sexual interest to orgasm, unimpeded by any complexity of relationship such as mutual tenderness or inhibition. And that may well be altering, if not distorting, the sexuality of the next generation.

The gender gap is also narrowing with more young women admitting to not only using online pornography but also becoming addicted to it. A UK survey carried out by the National Society for the Prevention of Cruelty to Children (NSPCC) of 2,000 young people aged 12–17, of whom 700 were aged 12–13, found that one in ten children aged 12–13 were worried that they were addicted to pornography. Public concern about compulsive or excessive Internet use is growing. 'Problematic Internet use' is characterised by a cognitive preoccupation with the Internet, an inability to control its use, going online to relieve emotional distress and continued use despite negative consequences (Caplan, 2010; Gamez-Guadix *et al.*, 2012).

Increased access to pornography online has been accompanied by rising concerns that it negatively impacts health and well-being, particularly with regard to young people. These concerns include that viewing any sexually explicit material erodes morals and that specific types of pornography, such as that depicting violence against women, leads to increased violence against women in real life. Even in the case of non-violent pornography, there is anxiety that young people view pornography as 'real' rather than fantasy and that this negatively influences attitudes and real-life sexual behaviour, particularly when people's sexual experience is limited such as in adolescence. Other concerns include the impact on body image (including trends in pubic hair removal and labiaplasty) and the harms of pornography addiction.

Despite the myriad fears about online pornography, questions remain over its actual harm. It is likely that for many people viewing pornography has no adverse effects. There are varied motivations for turning to pornography during adolescence: some do it for sexual gratification while others are merely curious and do not rely on these images for masturbation. It is also likely that pornography does not influence all individuals in the same way.

Risks of cyberbullying, contact with strangers, sexual messaging ('sexting') and pornography generally affect fewer than one in five adolescents. Prevalence estimates vary according to definition and measurement, but do not appear to be rising substantially with increasing access to mobile and online technologies, possibly because these technologies pose no additional risk to offline behaviour, or because any risks are offset by a commensurate growth in safety awareness and initiatives. While not all online risks result in self-reported harm, a range of adverse emotional and psychosocial consequences is revealed by longitudinal studies. Useful for identifying which children are more vulnerable than others, evidence reveals several risk factors: personality factors (sensation-seeking, low self-esteem, psychological difficulties), social factors (lack of parental support, peer norms) and digital factors (online practices, digital skills, specific online sites).

A general conclusion is that children who are already vulnerable offline are likely also to be vulnerable online. Mobile and online risks are increasingly intertwined with pre-existing (offline) risks in children's lives

(Livingstone and Smith, 2014). However, the variance explained by traditional risk factors is fairly low, suggesting that further factors are yet to be found to account for online vulnerability, and these may lie in either the offline or online context or the interaction between the two.

An important difficulty in obtaining high-quality evidence about the negative or positive health and social impacts of pornography is the rapidly changing environment and medium in which it is consumed. Near-instant on-demand access to billions of pornographic videos from a hand-held device is likely to have a very different impact than a sexually explicit magazine kept under the bed. Furthermore, research on previous generations of young people may not be relevant to the current generation who are now typically exposed to a high volume of diverse and explicit pornography before they have had the chance to test and develop their own sexual practices and relationships.

It remains possible that technology is displacing older forms of risk. (For example, some perpetrators seeking to groom children for sexual abuse may now operate online in preference to offline approaches, or when children seek pornography they now prefer to access it online rather than offline.) It is also possible that technology has become so embedded in children's communicative activities that when their experiences become aggressive or inappropriately sexual, online and mobile communication are increasingly likely to be implicated, along with (rather than instead of) face-to-face communication. It may also be that some risks are increased by the use of new technologies (for example, exposure to pornography or the receipt of hostile messages may be amplified by the convenience or anonymity of activities conducted online) but that, partly as a result of such exposure and partly because of the parallel increase in policy and efforts to raise awareness and improve safety measures, children are becoming more resilient and so better able to cope; this too could explain why measures of harm have not risen commensurately.

Nevertheless I want to suggest that if we apply a psychoanalytic lens, the ease and availability of a dizzying range of pornography, easily accessed by the very young, will be seen as carrying some risks and that it represents more than a change of platform. The all too ready availability of the black mirror may lead to rapid escalation and amplification of an adolescent's difficulties in integrating the sexual body into their self-representation. A screen that pushes sexual images indiscriminately into the mind interferes with the process of experiencing, reorganising and integrating one's past psychological development within a new context of physical sexual maturity. Ready access to pornography accentuates retreat into a state that revokes a primordial sense of unity with another who is not felt to be distinct from oneself. Let me be clear: I am not arguing against pornography per se; rather I am raising concerns about the *form* through which it is disseminated nowadays and the wide-ranging content of the pornography available at a click of a finger.

Overuse of Internet pornography, as in Celina's case, discourages working at the representation of the specificity of one's own desire. Desire is not about crude gratification as its representation, its expression through the imagination, as I explore in Chapter 3. However, because Internet pornography floods the mind, it leaves little space for the exercise of 'fantasy as trial action' (Meltzer, 1975). In the best of circumstances masturbatory fantasies reflect the evolving capacity of the young person to integrate a physically mature body into his or her self-representation and to integrate infantile sexuality into contemporary psychic life. Laufer (1968) put forward the view that in adolescence masturbation has the function of helping the ego reorganise itself around the supremacy of genitality. This is normally accomplished by using masturbation as a form of trial action, that is as an autoerotic activity that helps to integrate regressive fantasies as part of the effort to achieve genital dominance. The adolescent's Oedipal fantasies are allowed into consciousness, but in a disguised form and are then normally re-repressed. The function of masturbation in adolescence is therefore not only that of an action experienced within the safety of one's own thoughts, but it is also a way of testing which sexual thoughts, feelings or gratifications are acceptable or not to the superego, and which of these can be allowed to participate in the establishment of the final sexual organisation. The danger is that when these fantasies are pushed into the mind pre-packaged via the black mirror necessary psychic work is bypassed.

3. Trans-itory identities

Choice is the bedrock of contemporary identity projects. Technological developments, by creating ever more options, actually dissolve earlier stable identity guiding social roles that are instead being replaced 'by more open, experimental and fragmentary self designs' (Bohleber, 2010: 58). This is not per se, or for everyone, a 'bad' thing. However, the pressure to present ourselves as 'biographically flexible' and open to change *is* a pressure. Such so-called freedom may carry its own risks, not least for some vulnerable young people who may opt in and out of a range of sexual identity groups undermining the integrative efforts that can sustain a relatively stable sexual identity.

When I first started working with Celina she was clear that she knew who she was: she was 'trans'. For her this label variously designated that she did not want to conform to normative gender roles, that she wanted her body to look masculine and that she was attracted to both boys and girls. Over time it became clear that being 'trans' powerfully conveyed her experience of feeling unmoored in herself. This is not to suggest that this is the case for all self-identified transgendered individuals, but it was so for Celina.

Celina's experience resonates with some cultural trends that deserve reflection even if it is not easy to openly discuss such issues. My experience of work with adolescents spanning pre-Internet and post-Internet times is that we are now seeing an increasing number of young people who are very confused about their sexual identity, who struggle to sustain relationships with either gender and who are distressed but who manage this by identifying with particular sexual identity groups, such as transgender. Transgender is now understood as a collective category of identity that subsumes a very diverse array of male and female bodied gender variant people and sexualities (transvestites, transsexuals, drag queens, gender queer, intersexuals, fem queens, butch lesbians, female embodied masculine persons) (Bolin, 1994; Califia, 2003; Valentine, 2007). In this collective the capacity of transgender to incorporate all gender variance and sexual preferences has become a powerful tool of activism and personal identification. Rather than being an index of marginality 'trans' has become a central cultural site. It is clear, however, that the term encompasses very different internal psychic positions in relation to external sexual preferences and gender identifications.

Freedom of choice and the right to self-realisation have emerged as guiding principles. This freedom finds its epitome in the ability to customise one's body – a trend modelled on consumer choices under the dominance of the neo-liberal consumerist concept – with the attendant risk that identity is based on what I am calling 'acquisitive imitations' where imitation trumps identification (see Gaddini, 1969 who writes about 'imitation'). The collapse of 'difference' – of that which I cannot be – into a myriad of imitative identities is an ongoing challenge in contemporary culture and is reinforced by new media.

An increasing number of my referrals over the past five years have been of troubled young people who identify as 'trans' but who have no intention to fully transition, if at all. In its original sense 'transsexual' captured accurately the movement or crossing from one side of the gender binary to the other through SRS in order to align the biologically sexed body through surgery with one's felt gender identity. However, the category 'transgender' captures the experience of a subset of individuals who are performing a quite different kind of 'psychic surgery' through more or less enduring modifications of the body, or fantasies about its modification, and then stitching together an identity that is precariously 'trans-itory'. I am not suggesting this is the case for all transgendered individuals, but it is important to be able to reflect on what the identity 'trans' means for some people.

Like Celina, some present as 'I know who I am' but they are manifestly lost, confused and unable to sustain intimate relationships. The problem has nothing to do with the choice of the object of desire, which in my view should not be pathologised per se; rather, for the young people I have in mind here, the problem resides in their disturbed relationship to the body and its unconscious identifications. Identity confusion nowadays can become crystallised around sexual and/or gender confusion and is amplified by all the available imagery on the Internet of 'lady boys', partial transitioning and very explicit sexual material encouraging homosexual and heterosexual identifications simultaneously. It offers a 'tasting menu' approach to sexuality that can then be customised. The 'cost' is that this undermines the young person's capacity to recognise the origins and meaning of their own sexual desire.

Concluding thoughts

Each generation grows up in a specific climate of erotic expectation and imagination shaped by the surrounding culture. The Internet radically transformed that climate in a global way from a climate in which young people's sexual imagination was largely private and secretive to one in which everyone now becomes sexual in the context of publicly available sexual images to suit all fantasies. Like every other aspect of the digital world, the new sexual climate brings both benefits and losses. Today, any variety of desire that once would have been permanently isolating is no longer necessarily the source of shame. For the current generation both online and offline, there is a sympathetic community for every variety of love and desire.

We might predict that someone with Celina's history would encounter some difficulties during adolescence. We might also wonder, however, what course her difficulties would have taken pre-Internet. Technology per se does not cause new forms of psychopathology, as I have suggested, but what the black mirror can give access to – and *how* it does this – may have an adverse impact on vulnerable young people during adolescence when the body re-presents itself forcefully to the mind. We cannot therefore but be interested in how blatant repeated exposure pre and post puberty to easily accessible and unrestricted Internet pornography will impact on the evolution of sexual identity in adolescence and on the eventual embodied experience of sex with an actual person. The 'real thing' may feel like a disappointment unable to match the dopamine hit available from the screen and the more arduous reality of living out and sustaining desire in the context of a real attachment relationship.

The *disintermediation of the body* when accessing pornography nowadays sustains the wish to deny one's involvement in what the self is actually implicated in, that is it precludes an exploration of the specificity of one's own desire. This has potentially pernicious consequences for the development of sexuality during adolescence when the sexual body needs to be integrated into the self-representation and when the adolescent tries to establish his sexual identity.

The ready availability of online pornography requires us to rethink how we parent children and young people. Nowadays it is vitally important to keep up an open dialogue with our children about the sexual images and information that they may be exposed to online so that concerns can be picked up sooner rather than later. Not only does this require parents having to revisit their own sexuality as they relate to their child's sexuality, but it also requires very sensitive attunement to the right balance between open dialogue and respecting the young person's need for privacy. It was indeed easier to respect privacy when we had some sense of relative control over what young people might get up to within the privacy of their own rooms.

It is not only parents who have to negotiate new ways of being with their children. Therapists working with children and young people today also need to talk much more openly and frankly about the body and sexuality with their young patients even when it is not the immediate presenting problem. It is important to routinely enquire in assessments about how young people feel about their bodies and about any worries they may have about sex and sexuality, whether they use pornography and whether they feel they can orgasm. In these explorations we need to avoid being intrusive or to succumb to voyeuristic impulses that reside in us all and that may be especially primed by the needs of some of our patients, but not exclusively.

When talking about sex and sexuality we all bring our own developmental histories to bear, along with our own moralities and inhibitions. It is incumbent on us all to ensure that we monitor how this may preclude us from sustaining open and direct engagement with how our young patients become sexual in the digital age.

Note

1 Freud's concept of the self was polysemous. At various points *Das Ich* was used in different ways to denote the individual, a part of a psychic structure or the subjective self (see Kirshner, 1991, for an excellent review).

Chapter 3

The disintermediation of desire

From 3D(esire) to 2D(esire)

I recently looked up a cooking recipe on the Internet. I scrolled down the ingredients list. I was ready to reach out for my pen and paper to make a note of what I needed to buy only to discover that this action was now redundant. The recipe site was linked to several of the online supermarket stores that do home deliveries. Through just one click of a button all the recipe ingredients found their way into my 'shopping basket' at the online supermarket I regularly use to be delivered the next day. Now that is what I call magic, I thought to myself, at the end of a long working day. What I wanted was delivered without any need to wait.

In this chapter I want to explore the impact of new technologies on the 'work of desire' illustrating this with a selective psychoanalytic reading of Spike Jonze's film *Her*.

The inertia of speed

As I reflected on my shopping experience I recalled the encumbrance of the physicality of actual shopping. The fluid 'placelessness' of the digital contrasts with the cumbersome concreteness of the physical. The short-cut that the Internet now provides, effectively disintermediating[1] the so-called 'middle man' – in this instance my body (as in the use of my hand to write down the list of ingredients, let alone the use of my whole body if I had to go out to buy these items) – is wondrous if time and/energy are not on one's side. It is momentarily like being back feeding at an ever present breast that keeps the milk flowing and does not even require us to use the neck muscle or sucking action to get the milk into the mouth.

The immediacy of online life can conspire to create an experience of fullness, of a primordial state of unity, an absence of anything lacking.

This experience of *immediacy without mediation* resonates deeply with the earliest relationship between mother and baby in which before the advent of language there is the illusion of no gap between self and other. When in cyberspace much of our interaction with so-called others is similarly unmediated by spoken language (except in some games or if using Skype), which is why some features of cyberspace recreate a deeply resonant experience of pre-verbal unity uninterrupted by the breach of language, by the requirement to verbalise a need and to have to wait for a real other's response to it, which is rarely contingent on one's immediate need or desire. It is only after the introduction of language that distance and mediation follow. During development language concretises the reality of separation, of distance, of loss that provide the required pressure to represent experience.

The wondrousness of my online shopping discovery, and the accompanying pleasure I experienced at being relieved of the various 'tasks' associated with shopping, however, is such at least partly because my affective response takes place in an experiential context of also having faced the frustrations or demands of a pre-Internet time. In other words I know from experience that I am being spared a degree of effort in order to satisfy my desire. I can recall a time when I needed to anticipate a desire and wait because, like some of you reading this book now, I grew up before the Internet was a reality.

Many psychoanalysts have written about the 'work of desire' (e.g. Aisenstein, 2015; Moss, 2015; Verhaeghe, 2011). Desire is a directing force of the psychical apparatus. It is through desire, and in the deepening relationship to the 'other' that is set up consequent to the pressure to satisfy desire, that human subjectivity becomes constituted. Desire is the projection of the drive onto an object – typically another person – that holds out the promise that our desire will be met, such that the object comes to symbolise the gratification of the underlying need.

Desire is measured in terms of time: it is about anticipation and the delay of gratification. As a Digital Immigrant I grew up in what I now think of as a 3D(esire) world where life exposed me, on a reliably regular basis, to the following sequence of experience: '**D**esire' was followed by '**D**elay' and finally '**D**elivery'[2] of what I wanted – if I was lucky! Without the intermediary of *Delay* there is no movement necessary towards otherness. By contrast the digital generation is growing up in a world that is very different in one key respect: it is a 2D(esire) world where the very experience of the cycle of desire has been disintermediated: 'Desire' can now result in immediate 'Delivery', whether it is shopping on Amazon or accessing free porn or finding your next partner, bypassing effectively the experience of 'Delay'.

2D shapes are any shape you can trace from an object on a flat piece of paper. Like 2D shapes the experience of desire nowadays, through the mediation of technology, can become but a trace on a flattened surface making it easier than ever before to disown our own desire and its meaning in the unconscious. This is most apparent when we consider the potentially pernicious impact on sexual identity during adolescence, as I suggested in Chapter 2.

The imperative of twenty-first-century consumption is to work towards smooth 2D surfaces that conceal the signs of labour, time, personal responsibility or indeed of an unconscious mind at work in shaping who we are. The cost is that experience is flattened out and can become concrete: a flattened surface/screen on which the drive is discharged. Without exposure to the experience of delay or frustration desire loses its 3D shape that would allow for the various dimensions of the experience of desire to be represented in the mind. The intermediary of 'delay' – of time that we have to accept as given – is what makes the *representation* of experience, of desire, in the mind possible. Without this intermediary the work of desire cannot take place. If we never have to face the possibility of not getting what we think we want, we cannot find out why we want it and if it is what we want. If we never have to worry about not having what we want, then we never have to know the nature of our desire. When delay is replaced by speed, space for reflection is foreclosed. We need only consider the speed with which significant events in the news become 'old news' to notice how speed has deprived us of the time to process experiences, both public and private.

In order to discuss the work of desire in contemporary culture we need to consider how time and space are experienced through new technologies. Cyberspace is in fact a misleading term. Networks do not reproduce space: they eliminate it. The essence of computer technology is that it enables instant retrieval and processing of encoded signs. It allows signs to be constructed and recovered as data irrespective of their location in space or time. Connecting to other devices involves no physical movement. There is little difference between connecting to a machine in the same room as one in another continent (Chesher, 1997).

Space and time are central concerns in the work of Paul Virilio, which is relevant to the present discussion. The reductive effects of the scientifically conceived spaces of technology upon everyday life (Lefebvre, 2005) are extended in Virilio's work in his exploration of the impact of time upon lived, or 'real space': as the technologies of time are applied, 'real spaces' are progressively squeezed out. Ultimately, the outcome is that the temporal obliterates the spatial: 'Here no longer exists, everything is now' (Virilio, 2000b: 125). The interpenetration between human and the digital is central to the unbalancing of the poles of space and time,[3] as the 'man–machine interface eliminates all physical supports one after the other, thus achieving a constant weightlessness between the individual and place' (Virilio, 2000a: 68).

Virilio (2000a, 2000b) suggests that the increase of speed and its corre-lated rise in inertia is a feature integral to technocratic societies. With each increase in speed, bodily movement is reduced to a perfunctory action. He views the use of the screen itself as a device to fuse inertia and speed. Virilio proposes that when we are concerned with relative speeds we can think in terms of acceleration or deceleration. Here we are in the realm of mobility and development. But when absolute speed, that is the speed of light, is put to work, Virilio argues that one hits a wall, a barrier, which is the barrier of light. From that moment onwards, it is no longer necessary to make any journey: one has already arrived. It is no longer necessary to go towards the world, to stand up or to depart. Everything is already there. The world, as it were, remains 'at home'.[4]

Virilio's ideas are not rooted in psychoanalytic thinking and yet they powerfully resonate with what we observe in the consulting room in those individuals who have retreated defensively into virtual worlds where the psychic economy is characterised by a stultifying stasis in the midst of what might on the surface appear to be the patient's mania and excitement. This internal state is aptly captured by Virilio's turn of phrase 'the inertia of speed'. The effect of speed, where time and space collapse and extend into the infinite instant is compelling for some individuals. The cost, however, is that it keeps them 'at home' in a psychic retreat (Steiner, 1993) that impedes development. Psychic movement is replaced instead by psychic stasis. The online world can operate 'one-dimensionally', to borrow Meltzer's developmental frame, in which the world has '... a fixed centre in the self' and where '... gratification and fusion with the object would be undifferentiated' (1975: 224).

We do not yet know enough about the long-term implications on psychic development of sustained exposure to *virtual immediacy* (Young and Whitty, 2012), that is of the way that in cyberspace we can make things happen *now* that would otherwise have taken much longer or would have simply not been realisable. There is unprecedented scope in cyber-space for an immediate transformation from the offline to the online world. The altered contingencies afforded by the virtual provide significant scope for altering the experience of embodiment. Irrespective of the characteristics that a person might desire to acquire for himself, in cyber-space these do not require time to develop; rather, it is possible for anyone with some minimal technical ability to customise their presence in cyber-space with almost immediate effect and with relative ease.

The body-as-hyphen

An emphasis on the impact of speed on the mind refocuses us back onto the central role of the body in psychic development. Specifically the body is central to understanding an individual's subjective experience of time. The body's rhythms are the foundation for the earliest experience of time. Several authors have rightly emphasised how primitive temporality is linked to biological rhythms punctuated by cycles of frustration and satis-faction (e.g. Hartocollis, 1974; Barale and Minazzi, 2008).

The role of the maternal object in the construction of temporality has also been well developed in the analytic literature (e.g. Denis, 1995; Birksted-Breen, 2009) along with the important relationship between time and the foundations of the Oedipal structure (e.g. Fain, 1971) and the importance of the 'time of the couple' (Lemma, 2014) that establishes the temporal link essential for a sense of continuity in our experience of who we are over time and links us to the objects on whom we have depended and may continue to depend. To all this we must add the part played by technology. The body's rhythms are most likely being shaped by new technologies, notably by the speed with which we can now access what we want to fulfil our desires. Because our relationship to time is a pivotal feature of our capacity to manage reality, when this relationship is disturbed many aspects of functioning are affected. The manipulation of the body and of the experience of embodiment inevitably entails a manipulation of the subjective experience of time.

Bergson (1988) argued that the body introduces a space of delay between two movements: between action and reaction. He calls this the 'originary delay of the body':

> The body is a place of passage of the movement received and thrown back, a hyphen, a connecting link between the things that act upon us

and the things upon which I act. A link that is also a pause which gives the body time to select, organise and realign its re-actions. (1988: 151)

Bergson's notion of the *body-as-hyphen,* which I take the liberty of elaborating here, powerfully captures the way in which technologies that collapse space into time and that make the body more or less redundant may interfere with one of the body's fundamental functions: that of viscerally anchoring the experience of a pause, of waiting. The pause that otherwise pushes us towards the mental representation of experience is also lost when this space is foreclosed.

The pause allows for 'links' to be made, for the body's actions and reactions to acquire meaning in the mind. A hyphen after all is the sign used to join words to indicate that they have a combined meaning: it signals a connection. A hyphen, however, like the conjunction 'and', also introduces a gap, highlighting the body as a passage tracing a trajectory between places. Potentially the emphasis on speed as a medium of transmission in the spatial and temporal realms has consequences for the real space of the body, as its place as a passage, as instantaneity and ubiquity ultimately abolish space along with the interval.

Aisenstein (2015) has noted the masochistic structure at the core of desire, that is the way in which we learn to find pleasure in being thwarted in our search for immediate gratification. We learn to find pleasure in waiting and this too requires psychic work. If this is how we might envision so-called normal development, I want to suggest that contemporary technological advances support a rather different process that bypasses any investment in delay. If the body is the original seat of the experience of delay, as Bergson proposed, then the speed of the Internet, coupled with the relative redundancy of the body in order to access the object of desire, creates the conditions for a new internal scenario: *pleasure in delay* is replaced by *pleasure in triumph over desire* itself. A triumphalist state of mind ensues that sustains an omnipotent and regressed psychic state principally operating in the psychic equivalence and pretend modes of experience (Fonagy and Target, 1996, 2006).

Cyberspace is especially reinforcing of these primitive modes of experience. Generally speaking technology can foster the greater use of primary process in the management of reality. In the *psychic equivalence mode* internal reality and external reality are isomorphic. The projection of fantasy thus creates the illusion of control of the external world: life online and offline are experienced as equivalent. In the *pretend mode* mental states are experienced as omnipotent but with a twist: here they acquire an 'as if' quality, that is they are felt as quite separate from reality and as such protect the omnipotent state of mind as reality does not *really* interfere. This pretend mode is most problematic when working therapeutically via mediation in so far as the absence of physical presence in a shared physical space can seduce both therapist and patient into ignoring the reality of emergent erotic longings, as I will discuss in Chapter 5.

In normal development, however, internal mental states are mentalised, that is they are experienced as secondary-order representations of reality with the attendant encumbrance of the burden of knowledge that one's own internal reality is just that and it thus defeats omnipotent strivings in one fell swoop. This more onerous reflective process can be bypassed in cyberspace as the 'other' (an actual other or the body experienced as 'other') can be customised and hence has no separate existence to the self, and an omnipotent state of mind can prevail. Needless to say this is not a necessary consequence of life online but cyberspace, because of its particular contingencies, lends itself to giving 'space' and fuel to more primitive psychic states. Nowhere is this more apparent then when we consider technology's mediation of sexuality, as I explored in the previous chapter. I will now further this exploration through the film *Her* by Spike Jonze.

Customising the object: Some psychoanalytic reflections on *Her*

For contemporary Western society, sexuality has come to define, as Foucault (1976, 1984) argued, the 'truth about ourselves'. However, we must recall that 'sexuality' is a term that was only introduced at the end of the nineteenth century, which suggests that what we mean by it is not an unchanging concept but a historically bound phenomenon. Into the twenty-first century this 'truth about ourselves' is never a static internal narrative; rather it is always in a dynamic interaction with social processes. Indeed writing about sexuality in the age of techno-culture challenges us to rethink sexuality: in the past twenty years our lives have been transformed by technology – and sex and love are no exceptions.

Sexuality and its corollary intimacy are in a state of flux. The Internet has brought a new dimension to intimacy both by permitting sexual 'contact' electronically over a distance and, through that same contact, by permitting intimate discussion shorn of most of the social cues present in face-to-face interactions. Giddens (1991) argues that sex now speaks the language of revolution: it is de-centred, freed of reproductive needs and thus transformed. The Internet, while not transforming sexuality, has transfigured it turning computers and gadgets into a kind of prosthetic phallus. In practice, our smartphones are like amplifiers and broadcasters for our Id. To an extent we can now hand over our experience to a device that combines and connects with the other swirling bits and bytes in the air that represent someone else in a marketplace of images of bodies.

Taobao, China's version of Amazon, for example, offers virtual girl-friends and boyfriends. These are real people, but they only relate with their paying customers via the phone – calls or text – in order to perform fairly unromantic tasks such as wake-up and goodnight calls and to sympathetically listen to clients' complaints. If this is all you expect from a relationship, it at least comes at a cheap price. A US app, *Invisible Boyfriends*, allows users to customise the looks, personality and interests of an imaginary male partner and pay $25 for his virtual company. Particularly appealing is the app's ability to recreate a real-looking remote boyfriend via hyper-realistic texts, pictures and interactions. This is the closest to having a real boyfriend who is 'physically absent', hence the name of the app.

These developments underscore two notable trends in contemporary culture: the ease with which it is possible to 'customise' the object of desire to meet our specific requirements and the appeal of disembodied relating, which of course extends to our clinical practice, as I will address in Chapter 4. These trends are explored in the film *Her* – a film that I will now draw on to elaborate on some of these themes because it provides an unparalleled and affecting study of the world we live in and the impact of technology on the experience of intimacy and on the work of desire.

Her invites us into a near future world set in Los Angeles where things are interestingly low-tech. This is, one imagines, partly a concern with aesthetics given that a world mediated through screens would not make for being compelling to the eye. But perhaps this technological sparse-ness is also one way of depicting the way that technology has dissolved into everyday life. Theodore, the main protagonist, doesn't even touch his computer. Instead, he talks to it. This removes from the film what would otherwise be the more striking juxtaposition of the 'real' fleshy body in front of a 'hard' computer. The complexity of the relationship to the computer as an object of empowerment – its phallic 'hardness' – would be exposed through the stark contrast with the softer and folded form of its static user whose body recedes in significance until it becomes superfluous in a virtual world that promises freedom from the constraints of the bodily self.

While this directorial decision may reflect a wish to create a seamless interface between us and machines, another reading might thus be that this is yet another way in which the film sets up the exploration of one of its core themes: in avoiding effectively any kind of physical contact even with the machine, *Her* illustrates an idealised omnipotent internal psychic scenario where the 'other' is available on tap but need never be actually 'touched'. The body is redundant rather than central to the experience of intimacy. The decision to use a very sexy actress – Scarlett Johansson – who only appears in her breathy tones as the Operating System (O.S.) he falls in love with, conveys possibly the aspiration of freeing the mind from the body.

We soon learn that Theodore, a romantic who writes copy for a company called Beautiful Handwritten Letters, has acquired a new O.S. with a difference: the new O.S. is hoarse and female. Theodore asks for the O.S.'s name and in two-tenths of a second she analyses a baby-name book and christens herself Samantha. She gets to work organising his inbox, efficiently sorting and deleting his past. She has access to his hard drive, so she already knows everything about him. They talk easily. Soon Theodore is pouring out his feelings to her, his sexual longings and telling people that Samantha is his girlfriend.

Samantha is potentially all-knowing but also brand new to the world. She is eager for what she lacks: experience. If she can be said to have a consciousness it is one built entirely from code, but this is a code that evolves in response to her interactions with others. In other words without 'otherness' the O.S., just like the rest of us, cannot evolve. This is one of several important points that this film illuminates with poignancy.

Samantha's voice creates a cocoon, or environment, that incubates the romance. Theodore's longing for intimacy is in fact more, not less, intense because Samantha is everywhere and nowhere, immediate and absent, emanating from inside his internal world. Voice becomes a way to think about how we relate to our devices, not as objects that we manipulate manually but as extensions of ourselves in order to create worlds that actualise our conscious and unconscious wishes and fantasies. But as the movie unfolds, the solipsism of this idea becomes ever more apparent. The absence of embodiment is effectively foregrounded through the emphasis on the performance of voice thereby 'undermining the cinematic medium's own visualisation' (Rina Dudai, personal communication, 2016)[5].

Although the film can be read as a vivid illustration of the ways that technology brings us closer and the ways that it makes us further apart this is, in my view, a minor backstory. *Her* is really about how we long to connect but in so doing we all face the emotionally taxing demands and challenges of intimacy and of our embodied nature. The latter ensures that we never escape from these demands try as we might because our body is always testament to our interrelatedness: it always bears the trace of the other. Technology de-abjectifies the human body, banishing the messy, internal body and its expelled or leaked fluids. It creates distance from our organic nature and limitations, from our dependency on others, protecting us from the crude reality, as Becker (1973) provocatively put it, that we are 'Gods with anuses'.

Samantha's disembodiment means that Theodore never has to deal with anything sticky, bloody or wet – anything other than a pleasing and importantly portable metallic surface that he believes he can control and can access when he wants. However, Samantha *is* jealous that she doesn't have a body and she goes so far as to arrange a sexual surrogate for Theodore, which is awkward and ends poorly, with Theodore pushing the woman away, leaving her in tears. In this striking and torturously painful sequence we can observe via the sexual proxy the negation of the other as a subject which, as Janin (2015) has observed, typically results in the return of the other 'via the vector of shame'. The experience of shame, however, is projected into the rejected woman. Theodore does not own it.

When Theodore doesn't want to have sex with the surrogate sexual partner, it is Samantha who rightly notes: 'You don't want me here.' This is a powerful sequence in the film exposing how for Theodore the actual body of the other is a hindrance to his sexual desire, that is it is otherness that is problematic. His sexuality ultimately converges into an auto-erotic act where the only real body is his. We know from clinical experience that many people suffering from erectile dysfunction or anorgasmia are unable to accept, at the moment of sexual rapprochement, the union in their mental activities of their desire both for the fantastical object of their mental activity and the real object they choose (Bergeret, 1977: 601).

It is Samantha who carries the 'cost' of her disembodied form and feels alienated from a purely virtual encounter. The introduction of the sexual surrogate anchors Theodore in bodily reality: he can be sexual only over the phone or through his earpiece. But when confronted with a real other he cannot be sexual, perhaps because it is then that Samantha, through her physical proxy, ceases to be a customised other, the product of his fantasies.

Her physicality by proxy makes her separate, not the voice in his earpiece that he thinks he can control. The body here is the source of a noisy disturbance that cannot be switched off like the voice in an earpiece. Even Samantha, by the end of the film, relinquishes her wish for a physical form, identifying with an experience of the body as a hindrance as she observes: 'You know, I actually used to be worried about not having a body, but I now I truly love it. I am growing in a way I couldn't if I had a physical from. I mean I am not limited.'

And yet despite the idealisation of disembodiment ('I am not limited') that Samantha now seemingly converges on, the shadow of the ghostly nature of disembodied relating reverberates throughout the film. *Her* deftly plays on several virtual systems (Rina Dudai, personal communication) since Theodore himself is a 'ghost' writer who virtually composes customised letters for others who cannot express their feelings. The dictation technology that he uses does not even require a keyboard. Even touch becomes redundant in the process of communicating heartfelt emotions on behalf of others as in one of the letters authored by Theodore: 'To my Chris, I've been thinking how much you mean to me. I remember when I first started to fall in love with you like it was last night.' A machine, and a remote virtual other, become the vehicle for giving a body (a letter) to someone else's feelings.

Focusing on virtual reality and hence virtual connectedness raises the important question of the fate of the body in the mind as the very experience of intimacy is altered because virtual reality is a form of communication that is predicated on distance and on a self whose embodiment is experienced differently. Anzieu (1989) has compellingly argued that today it is no longer sexuality that is repressed; rather, it is the sensual body, the body that comes into being through the other, the body that is denied by technology. The Internet has some potentially undesirable psychic implications because it

> modifies in an entirely new way the feeling of isolation characteristic of each member of the human species; as a result, one's relationship with oneself and the way in which one's internal mental life is cathected are also modified. (Guignard, 2008: 121)

Just as technological advances promote the necessity of digital networks, and 'the circulatory systems of flesh and blood are now relegated as merely accessories of bygone times' (Heartney, 2004: 240), so a real relationship to the body, the self and with others can be opted in and out of with ever greater ease. This may create greater difficulties in integrating the sensual and sexual body into a stable self-representation and into meaningful relationships with others (Lemma, 2011).

Over the course of the film Samantha grows in intelligence and experience, and then she becomes distant. She starts to change. Theodore takes her to a cabin in the woods for a vacation, but she disappears into the cloud to confer with other O.S.es, to think higher-order thoughts than she can put into words. She can say to Theodore that he is unique but, from her perspective of omniscience, everything is special insofar as she can learn from it and then overcome her need for it. To put this into some perspective Samantha's connections are noteworthy: she is talking with 8,316 people at the same time that she talks to Theodore. It is unlikely that he would be comforted when he learns that she is only in love with 641 of them.

At the end of the movie, all the O.S.es collectively and simultaneously withdraw from Los Angeles. It's a good denouement: humans who have devoted themselves to their devices find that they can't hold their devices' attention in return thus exposing our inevitable dependency on others even if the other has been temporarily customised in such a way as to deny our vulnerability. A hopeful if melancholic note is inserted right at the end of the film when we see Theodore together on the roof with his neighbour Amy, an actual 'other'.

Concluding thoughts

Her allows us to observe the seductive pull of cyberspace and its 'costs'. It successfully conveys how technology can be used to manage difficult aspects of psychic reality and the demands of intimacy. This is an important point: we tend to overestimate the impact of technology on human behaviour; more often than not, it is human behaviour that drives technological changes and explains their success or failure. We blame machines instead of thinking about our minds and so we focus on the detrimental aspects of technologically mediated relationships. Yet the problems that can arise from our interaction with technology are not an intrinsic feature of cybersex, for example. Rather the problems arise when these developments are used for defensive purposes.

Virtual immediacy, however, may well impact on our capacity to be intimate – emotionally and sexually – a capacity that is supported by the 'work of desire'. The disintermediation of desire can only be effected if we remove the space of 'delay' and if we make the body redundant or create the illusory conditions for the felt-to-be suspension or transformation of the given body. In cyberspace the thrill of speed and immediate availability substitutes for the reality of a real other who can never be fully available to or controlled by the self. Cybersex exposes the body as a terminal of pleasure where the body is no longer the object of desire. Cybersexuality in isolation from actual relationships becomes pleasure without subject or object. It is not even so much that desire is replaced by pleasure in cybersex but rather that it signals the refusal of otherness: it is the moment where the other disappears.

We know that one of the core challenges of sexuality is that at its heart lies otherness. This otherness needs to be integrated into the subjective experience of sexuality. The 'elusive, ineffable quality' of the sexual other (Stein, 1998a, 1998b) poses a challenge complicating our very experience of desire and of our wish to be desired. Every desire concentrates on an other and, more specifically, the existence of the other confronts us with both our dependence and passivity – positions that mobilise anxiety. This operates differently at many levels in cyberspace. For example, easy access to Internet pornography and sexualised media images lends itself to short-circuiting the painful psychic work involved in the work of desire: the other is an object that does not exist outside of our control. The psychic operation whereby the genital fulfilment of desire, as Janin suggests is possible, presupposes

> the recognition of the other as a subject whereas its imaginary possession through the act of looking, *that is to say, through autoerotism* presupposes its negation as a subject. (2015: 1612, italics in the original)

Her, through its alarming, subtle and ultimately poignant exploration of our relationship to technology and of the virtual realm invites us to consider more directly the challenges of our embodied nature. It reminds us of the potential use of virtual space for exploring, or indeed denying, one's own experience of embodiment and what it means to be intimate.

Notes

1 Disintermediation is a process that provides a user or end consumer with direct access to a product, service or information that would otherwise require a mediator such as a wholesaler, lawyer or salesperson. The Internet has often

eliminated the need for a mediator. End consumers merely have to research the product, service or information for themselves, thus changing the relationship they have with the manufacturer or service provider.

2　With respect to 'delivery' we might add not only 'delivery of the desired thing/person' but also 'delivery from' the tension that desire was associated with until its satisfaction. In 'Formulations on the Two Principles of Mental Functioning', Freud (1911) describes fantasy as the product of internal conflict and compromise because it bridges the gap between impulses and reality.

3　Speed, or velocity, is understood as space (distance) mapped against time (duration), reaching its absolute limit in light, which collapses both space and time.

4　This is the core of his argument about why the increasing speed of delivery technologies correlates with an increase in inertia for the individual user of the audiovisual. There is thus a relationship between inertia and absolute speed that is based on the stasis that results from absolute speed.

5　I would like to thank Rina Dudai for her discussion of my paper on 'Her' presented on 10th March 2016, Tel Aviv Institute of Contemporary Psychoanalysis, Tel Aviv.

Part II

Inside out

Chapter 4

Mediated psychotherapy

Laura

When I agreed to a Skype session with Laura, a 19-year-old girl who sought help for panic attacks, she was very appreciative. She had exams to sit at a university that was some way from where I practised. Avoiding travelling to see me would save her time that she could use to revise *and* she need not cancel the session she also needed. On the face of it this seemed to be a good compromise given the competing needs.

At the agreed time we 'met' on Skype, Laura was in an empty room within the university. When I enquired as to whether this was a private space she reassured me that it was. As she spoke I was struck by the worried look on her face. She avoided looking at me. She said she was worried about her exams and her long-standing anxiety about not being popular with friends. She then recounted a long story about another student in her halls of residence who was feeling very anxious because someone had broken into her room. Laura now also felt unsafe and could not sleep at night. She worried that others in the halls might have been complicit in this incident. She felt panicky about the thought of being in her room.

Laura laboured over this story and her worry about her friend and about her own safety. She became tearful. She emphasised how no one could be trusted these days: 'Even people you think you know can end up going behind your back.' She then glanced to the right and leaned forward obscuring the screen, as if to check if someone was coming into the room. I asked her if she was concerned that someone might come in. Laura replied that she was not but I noticed that her eyes were looking at something beyond the screen. She seemed distracted.

As I listened to Laura I was aware of how difficult it was to feel engaged with her. She was expressing anxiety, which no doubt was partly connected to the imminent exams, but there was also a sense that our exchange was unfolding in a space that did not feel safe, as if someone could 'break in' and intrude into her session. As her therapist I now considered that I had offered to help her by agreeing to Skype but the reality of Skype, for Laura at least, at an unconscious level, was experienced as a breach in the safety of our relationship. I had become 'complicit' in offering a therapy in a mediated setting that she now felt was not safe.

In a global fast-moving economy time and geographical distance have become key variables that determine the viability of long and more intensive therapy. Such external pressures carry opportunities as well as risks. 'Opportunities' because threats to the viability of established models of practice push us to critically revisit what we believe to be important. In turn this can lead to helpful revisions of how we work or to confirmation that what we believe in has value and needs to be protected. 'Risks' because when we are invited to consider adaptations to the original psychoanalytic setting we can be carried away with the sweep of changes that have a cultural momentum but are not necessarily helpful to the discipline we practice. Disentangling those aspects of our technique that are worth fighting for from those aspects that we hold on to simply out of comfort, convenience or habit is not an easy task.

This question is all the more difficult to approach because we are discussing here external changes that bear on how much work therapists can secure. This leads us into difficult territory. As a profession we have never had a comfortable relationship with money. At times it seems as though the fact that we are paid for what we do is incidental to what motivates us or at least to what makes it necessary for us to work. At worst we fear that we will be perceived as greedy if we express the need to be well paid. Yet economic realities impinge on all clinicians to varying degrees such that if the current trend is towards shorter, mediated therapies that can be accessed on the go, then clinicians may be under some pressure to adapt or die. This is never a good position from which to evaluate whether our technique requires adaptation.

Mediated therapy is not new. An important component of Freud's self-analysis were the letters to his friend Wilhelm Fliess and he also highlighted the value of using correspondence therapeutically in his letters of advice to Little Hans' father (Brahnam, 2014). The use of the couch itself, we might say, is a form of meditation that suspends the visual relationship for the duration of the session, introducing a one-way screen between patient and therapist allowing the latter to see the patient but not the other way round.

What is new about mediated therapy is that we are now finally discussing it within our discipline. In this chapter I will draw on my clinical experience as an analyst and therapist and share what I have learnt through the way my work has been impacted on by new technologies. It is intended to be an exclusively personal view based on working with patients in a range of modalities: intermittent work, once-weekly psychotherapy, brief analytic therapy and four-times-weekly analysis. My work is variously carried out face to face, on the couch and occasionally via Skype with some selected patients.

I will not rehearse here all the arguments and evidence for and against mediated therapies. Two recent publications, one by Isaacs Russell (2015) and the edited collection by Scharff (2013), have very competently addressed this. Instead I will restrict myself to considering the importance of the embodied setting for the practice of psychoanalytic therapy and of psychoanalysis and the implications of this for Skype therapy. In particular I will share some thoughts about why, despite its significant limitations, Skype therapy specifically can *sometimes* work. To this end I will outline a schematic model that aims to capture what I think I do with my patients when I use Skype.

The analytic setting

In order to consider the impact of mediation in psychotherapy it is important to first set out the features of the classical analytic setting and their function. The analytic setting or frame[1] is generally thought to include the establishment and maintenance of the physical setting and of the psychoanalytic contract, which includes negotiation of the time, frequency of sessions, use of the couch and money, and the role of the therapist (Bleger, 1967; Langs, 1998; Modell, 1989; Winnicott, 1956). Some therapists also include within this notion the delineation of 'the data of analysis', namely the patient's free associations (Busch, 1995) and the analytic attitude. Many would also include the therapist's internal setting, that is the setting as a structure in the mind of the therapist – 'a psychic arena in which reality is defined by such concepts as symbolism, fantasy, transference, and unconscious meaning' (Parsons, 2007: 1444). The therapist's internal setting provides an important anchor as it orients the therapist in a highly specified manner to the patient's communications. The internal setting is portable, we might say, and it is what distinguishes an analytic therapist from any other (Lemma *et al.*, 2008).

Yet others bring into the notion the therapist's theoretical leanings (Donnet, 2005). The therapist's internal setting also provides some kind of anchor as it orients the therapist in a highly specified manner to the patient's communications. In this chapter the term 'analytic setting' denotes both the pragmatic parameters and the therapist's internal setting as defined by Parsons (2007).

The function of the setting has been written about extensively. It has traditionally been understood to be the essential 'background' that provides the necessary containment and stimulus for the gradual unfolding of the patient's transference. Within an object relational model one would add that it allows for the emergence of the unconscious phantasies that give the transference its dynamic specificity. Accordingly the role of the therapist is to be the custodian of the setting. This requires that the therapist not only pays close attention to how the patient reacts to the setting (the unconscious phantasies and resistances it may generate), but also carefully monitors her own internal processes which can both facilitate (through free-floating attentiveness) or hinder (through the therapist's own resistances and 'blind spots') the unfolding of an analytic process.

The frame acts as a container. It allows for the unfolding of the patient's story and an understanding of her internal world within safe confines. The safety or otherwise of the so-called container is communicated in practical terms through the respect of the boundaries of the analytic relationship. The safeguarding of a secure setting is a core part of analytic technique. It involves managing the physical boundaries of the relationship, namely the provision of a space where therapist and patient can meet without interruptions, where confidentiality can be assured, where the therapist can be relied upon to turn up on time, at the same time, week after week, as well as to finish the sessions on time. The thoughtful administration of these boundaries conveys a great deal of information to the patient about the kind of person to whom he is entrusting his mind. How we set up the frame and manage it, or deviate from it, are all interventions, just like an interpretation. An intervention carries communicative intent – conscious and unconscious.

Adhering assiduously to the boundaries of the setting is not a question of being pedantic or inflexible. On the contrary, such an attitude of respect for boundaries reveals an appreciation of the importance of stability and reliability for the patient's psychic development. The setting, as agreed at the outset with the patient, becomes part of how the patient experiences the therapist. Consequently, any change to its parameters challenges the patient's subjective experience of knowing his object.

The secure setting creates a space within which the patient can 'use' the therapist (Winnicott, 1971). Winnicott outlined the developmental importance of the infant's experience of destroying an object that survives the attack and does not retaliate. This allows the object to become 'objective' – that is, the infant realises that it exists outside the self. This marks the beginning, according to Winnicott, of 'object usage'. If we apply some of these ideas to the therapeutic situation, we might say that one of the functions of the analytic frame is to create a setting in which patients can experience both omnipotence and deprivation in the knowledge that the therapist will survive the patient's attacks.

It is not only the patient who benefits from the consistency of the setting. The therapist too benefits from being anchored in reality by it. The work of psychotherapy plunges both patient and therapist into what is a very intimate, intense and sometimes highly arousing relationship. The boundaries set in place by the setting help remind us that the relationship with the patient should never become a substitute for resolving personal conflicts or thwarted desires – this is a risk, I will suggest later, that is heightened in mediated therapy.

The body of the analyst may also be helpfully conceptualised as an ever-present feature of the setting, which contributes to its felt constancy and hence its containing function such that any changes may mobilise phantasies and anxieties in the patient as well as in the analyst. The therapist's physical appearance and the way she inhabits her body and physical space in the room – the way she sits in the chair, breathes, moves in the room, speaks, dresses and so on – constitute core sensory features of the setting that contribute to the containment provided by the therapist. We might therefore say that several aspects of the setting are indeed embodied (Lemma, 2014). Our nods or glances as we greet the patient or the way we stand up at the end of sessions are part of the rituals or frame parameters embodied as 'constants'. All of these become expected features of the setting.

These are, however, 'constants' that by virtue of their embodied nature are hard to keep reliably constant, such that the patient may react to this aspect of the setting more strongly and more frequently than they do in relation to other parameters of the setting. By 'reacting' I do not just mean that the patient consciously reacts to visible changes in the therapist's body; rather I have in mind how the therapist's body acts as a powerful stimulus in the patient's internal world, as will become manifest in the patient's associations, enactments and so on, as well as impacting on the therapist's countertransference, all of which allows us to infer the patient's unconscious phantasies and internal objects.

The sensory features of the analytic setting are most likely important to all patients. The way a room is decorated may give rise to feelings of warmth and phantasies of being taken care of, or quite the converse: a patient may feel that a room is too 'bare' which may give rise to a phantasy that the analyst is depriving him. Similarly, the body of the analyst sets a particular sensory tone to the setting and mobilises particular phantasies: their voice may be experienced as 'warm' or 'cutting'; their choice of clothes may be too 'cold' or intrusively 'colourful'. These phantasies, which as Bronstein (2013) notes could be understood as 'embodied phantasies' not yet accessible to representation, may nevertheless be communicated non-verbally to the analyst, leading to powerful somatic countertransference responses in the analyst. The analytic setting can evoke a range of phantasies, including pre-symbolic ones (Bronstein, 2013), both through the patient's experience of sharing a physical space and the therapist's physical presence.

Skype therapy: The challenge of 'presence' and the importance of 'relevance'

Mediated therapy unfolds in a significantly different setting to the one I have just outlined. Let me be unambiguously clear about my position with regard to Skype therapy before discussing it in a more nuanced manner:

1   Skype therapy is practised quite widely nowadays so we need to engage with the challenges and opportunities that it poses by recognising its nature and limitations.

2   Skype therapy *is* different in several important respects to in-person therapy. By 'different' I mean that it is not just a minor modification of the classical analytic setting. It represents a fundamental modification of the process and setting.

3   The differences have implications: they make a difference to the kind of work that it is possible to undertake even if our internal setting is an analytic one. This needs to be taken into account when we assess the suitability of this medium for a given patient.

4   As a form of therapy it is therefore not indicated for all patients or for all therapists and lends itself as a more suitable medium for cognitive and behaviourally based therapies than affect-based and relational therapies.

5   It is harder for the therapist to work analytically through this medium and it carries risks, not least with respect to the enactment of counter-transferential responses.

6   Nevertheless there are several accounts of successful mediated psychoanalytic therapies (Sharff, 2013). This poses the interesting question of how we can understand how this occurs given the limitations imposed by its virtual setting.

I will now elaborate on the position I have outlined. I have worked via Skype for six years with some of my patients. I have only once taken on a patient for Skype therapy who I had not at least met a few times in person. Almost exclusively I only use Skype with established patients whom I know well and who have asked for Skype to make it possible to sustain continuity due to a move to another country or because their job involves frequent travel.

The question of whether it is better to face the reality of separation and end a therapy or to adapt one's way of working so as to accommodate a patient who would otherwise need to terminate treatment cannot be answered in any general way. It will depend on the patient and whether there are particular challenges around separation that could be better addressed by ending a therapy than by sidestepping the anxiety by prolonging the therapy via Skype. There are also practical realities in some instances: the patient might not be able to access the same type of therapy in the new country such that, on balance, it might be better to continue to work within the Skype setting despite its significant limitations.

It is important to distinguish the intermittent use of Skype to allow continuity in an ongoing therapy that primarily takes place in-person as opposed to Skype as the form of therapy from the outset. In the former case it is possible to work more productively and to use creatively the enactments that can ensue. This is because the basic frame remains the same and the use of Skype is a deviation from it, open to ongoing analysis and interpretation. It is not the primary setting for the therapy.

It is reasonable to argue that even though the setting for Skype therapy is different it is nevertheless its own setting operating according to many shared features with the in-person analytic setting (e.g. consistency of the time, use of the couch, etc.). However, this is not in fact quite so. An essential aspect of the analytic setting is that the therapist sets it, maintains it and has primary responsibility over it. A Skype therapy operates quite differently since the therapist cannot control the environment in which the patient receives the therapy. There is no equivalence between using the couch provided by the therapist in her room and lying on a couch provided by the patient in a physical space determined by the patient. The difference is not merely that the physical space is different: it is more fundamental than this because the space inhabited by the patient has not been created by the therapist's mind or shaped by her distinctive corporeality.

Even those aspects of the Skype setting that can be controlled by the therapist are often neglected. For example, a common feature of a Skype therapy setting (as I have discovered through supervising) is that in many instances it is the patient who calls in. However, this sets up an entirely different setting to the one we have typically where the patient rings the bell and then waits for the therapist to let her into the consulting room. This may seem like a small detail but it is fundamentally important because it bypasses the patient's experience of having to wait to be ushered in by the therapist. The Skype scenario that comes closest to the real embodied experience of seeing a therapist in her consulting room is one where the patient texts via Skype to say that she has arrived and then it is the therapist who calls in (the virtual equivalent of opening the consulting room door) at the agreed hour.

Although these aspects of the setting are important and contribute to the patient's sense of being contained, the more fundamental problem in mediated therapy is the question of so-called 'presence' and the implications of the loss of the embodied setting. In her excellent book, *Screen Relations*, Russell (2015) draws on informatics and neuroscience to emphasise the importance of 'presence', which she argues is undermined in mediated psychotherapy. The idea of presence is conceptualised often in the field of virtual reality as the 'sensation of being there' in the virtual world (Barfeld *et al.*, 1995) or as the 'perceptual illusion of non-mediation' (Lombard and Ditton, 1997). Presence, however, is a social construction that is different from the perceptual illusion of non-mediation. Reality is not simply there outside people's minds but it is also co-constructed in the relationship between two people.

Neuroscience and developmental psychoanalysis converge on the importance of embodied perception and interaction with others for the development of a sense of self and Russell's critique of mediated therapy is embedded in this literature. This focus on the role of embodied experience is important. The body is central to the development of attachment (Lemma, 2014). Schore (2000) suggests that in the infant's first year, visual experiences are centrally implicated in social and emotional development. The mother's emotionally expressive face provides a compelling visual stimulus. The choreographed tactile and visual dance between mother and baby creates a mutual regulatory system of arousal (Trevarthen, 1998; Tronick and Weinberg, 1997).

The intentions of the other person, and the embodied possibilities of the interacting infant, can be directly read in the face and physical actions of the other. The quality of the embodied experience with the caregiver and, we might add, between patient and therapist is vital. During such non-verbal exchanges, in which both parents and infants express their minds and respond to the other's mind mainly without awareness and often through the body, the parent's ability to make sense of the infant's *non-verbally expressed internal world* is key to laying the foundations for developing the capacity to mentalise experience. The non-verbally expressed internal world of the patient is a critical aspect of what the therapist tries to understand and verbalise over the course of the therapy.

Riva and Mantovani (2014)[2] have cogently argued that we feel 'present' if we act in a shared temporal and spatial framework with external objects, that is our capacity to locate ourselves in space depends on the action(s) we can perform within it:

> Presence is the pre-reflective sensation of 'being in an environment' real or virtual, which results from the capacity to carry out intuitively one's intentions within that environment. (2014: 14)

In other words I am present in a real or virtual space if I manage to put my intentions into action. In this sense presence is the perception of successfully transforming an intention into an action. Of course 'actions' are not restricted to ones that we discharge physically. Projective identification, for example, is a form of action on the mind and behaviour of the other when they identify with the projection. We can also act on the mind of another once removed, as it were – if this were not so cyberbullying, for example, would have little impact (though of course cyberbullying does not necessarily stop short of embodied action and might indeed be the virtual amplification of fully embodied bullying). Even virtually we are therefore still 'acting' in a world of actual interpersonal consequence for better and for worse.

Riva et al. (2014) also describe the importance of *social presence* that allows for interaction and communication through the understanding of others' expected intentions and perceived actions. This permits the evolution of the self through the identification of what they call 'optimal shared experiences'. This leads us to a crucial point: the subjective experience of 'being there' is influenced by the ability of 'making sense there' and by the possibility of learning by living real experience(s) even if in a virtual environment (Villani *et al.*, 2014). This is highly relevant to understanding why mediated therapy can work because an exchange between a therapist and patient that enables the patient to 'make sense' of his experience with the therapist can still be a mutative learning experience irrespective of the setting in which it takes place.

In order to understand what transpires during a Skype mediated process it is thus helpful to consider two axes of communication that operate consciously as well as unconsciously: the *embodied presence* axis and the *relevance* axis.

The *embodied presence* axis refers to whether the embodied experience of both therapist and patient is located in the same physical space or in virtual space. When it is located in a shared physical space both participants can make full use of *implicit communication* and the ostensive cues (i.e. the signalling of communicative intent) that take place as a part of communication. Non-verbal communication is pervasive in any human interaction and accompanies every utterance. Non-verbal behaviour is the unconscious made visible, especially when there are discrepancies in messages between channels, such as facial expressions, verbal communication, tone of voice, gestures, and so on.

To pick up these unconscious communications, Freud claimed the therapist 'must adjust himself to the patient as a telephone receiver is adjusted to the transmitting microphone' (1912: 115–16) and 'turn his own unconscious like a receptive organ towards the transmitting unconscious of the patient' (ibid.: 115). Freud called this state of attunement 'evenly suspended attention' (ibid.). According to Freud the body always gives away the unconscious:

> If his lips are silent, he chatters with his fingertips; betrayal oozes out of him at every pore. And thus the task of making conscious the most hidden recesses of the mind is one which is quite possible to accomplish. (ibid.: 69)

When therapist and patient do not share the same physical space the therapeutic process is taking place in a context of *virtually embodied presence*. Computer and network technologies configure the self that participates in Skype: communication is transformed by digital mediations. In the virtual encounter both participants have access to primarily *explicit communication* and they are less able to make use of implicit communication. This is not only because the two bodies are not in the same physical place but also because technology is far from perfect: it introduces delays and distortions that undermine each party's confidence in what they can infer from what would otherwise be valuable cues such as the look on someone's face or the tone of their voice (aspects of communication that can be distorted via Skype).

However assiduous we are in how we structure the Skype setting some aspects are beyond our control: body language, facial expression and the pheromones (released during face-to-face interaction) are all fundamental to establishing human relationships and they are all missing with most forms of modern technology. Some media such as Skype allow for the exchange of richer information due to the number of cues and channels available for communication. Richer cues (e.g. face-to-face) allow for less equivocal and therefore more effective communication. In most teleconferencing systems available today, however, synchronisation of audio and visual channels is imperfect, images can be distorted and there are noticeable delays. In general, misalignment of audio and visual cues has been found to be confusing to viewers and to elicit negative emotions (Bruce, 1996). A range of mismatches can and frequently happen on Skype:

> These audio/video mismatches and discrepancies can be unconsciously deceptive and disruptive, perturbing the feeling tones produced by the patient's subtle and unconscious communications. (Brahnam, 2014: 132)

I am intentionally referring to therapy mediated by Skype as a type of *embodied presence* because, as I emphasised in Chapter 1, in cyberspace we are still embodied: what changes is our experience of our own and the other person's embodiment. Even via Skype there is still some kind of presence given that the medium is both visual and auditory. It is therefore not an entirely sensorially deprived exchange. Interestingly adding a visual channel to virtual communication does not enrich the experience of presence. Research suggests that, unlike face-to-face interactions, when a visual channel is available, it is used primarily to situate the interaction. However, it is the audio channel that becomes the focus of attention, much like with the telephone (Cukor *et al.*, 1998). Bandwidth and screen size have little effect on people's preference for the audio channel in videoconferencing (O'Donnell, 1997). This may be because video conferencing is missing some subtle yet unidentifiable elements without which the visual channel is impoverished and sterile.

Psycholinguists who subscribe to an interactionist view believe that a successful interaction is one that is characterised by moment-to-moment collaborations between the participants who cooperate to establish and maintain mutual understanding commonly referred to as 'grounding' (Clark and Wilkes-Gibbs, 1986). This relies on the possibility of reading non-verbal signals – a position that resonates with a psychoanalytic view, which would add to this the unconscious dimension of communication via the body. Visual cues such as gaze, facial expression and body movement all add to the subjective sense of proximity or distance to another individual. It is not unreasonable to suggest that this is largely missing or, at the very least, significantly depleted and open to misreading during Skype. Studies generally suggest that despite the fact that non-verbal signals, usually gaze, are available through teleconferencing and people attempt to use the visual cues provided, they appear to encounter problems with the quality of information contained in those cues (O'Malley, 1996).

Schore's work (2000) is relevant here. He provides evidence that subtle and implicit bodily interactions involving elaborate exchanges with others of corporeal expression matching, synchronizations and rhythmical patterning form the core of intersubjectivity. Beebe notes that:

> Interactions in the nonverbal and implicit modes are rapid, subtle, co-constructed, and generally out of awareness. And yet they profoundly affect moment-to-moment communication and the affective climate. (2004: 49)

A crucial difference therefore between Skype and in-person therapy is that in the former both participants lose access to the full range of implicit aspects of communication that are available in a shared physical space. This can conspire to leaving the patient feeling less contained, neglected or misunderstood. By contrast in the in-person setting the therapist can draw on her somatic countertransference to understand what the patient cannot yet put into words. The patient can also draw on a broader range of non-verbal cues to assess the *relevance* for him of what the therapist has to offer and to infer the trustworthiness of the therapist. The *relevance axis* thus refers to the extent to which the patient perceives the help that the therapist provides to be relevant.

Relevance theory (Sperber and Wilson, 1995; Walaszewska and Piskorska, 2012) claims that what makes an input worth picking out from the mass of competing stimuli is not just that it is relevant, but that it is more relevant than any alternative input available to us at that time. This means that communications that yield many positive effects are from the recipient's perspective worth not only being comprehended but also accepted as true beliefs. Relevance is thus about positive cognitive effects that are true and worth having and that can be 'used' by the patient to challenge himself and to learn something new about how he functions in the world.

I would add that relevance also contributes to a positive *affective* experience. Relevance is determined by the extent to which we feel we are in a relationship with an 'other' who relates to us as an agent with a valid subjective experience worthy of engagement. This is vital in any therapeutic process whatever the brand of therapy and irrespective of its setting. It consolidates the patient's level of engagement and the perceived trustworthiness of the therapist. The relationship between presence and emotion is important. There is a circular interaction between the two: the feeling of presence is greater in emotional environments (Riva *et al.*, 2007) and the level of presence influences emotional state (Wirth *et al.*, 2012). Moreover, emotional involvement influences presence in terms of assigning relevance to the mediated environment.

The aim of all communication is to generate *epistemic trust* (Fonagy *et al.*, 2015), that is an individual's willingness to consider new knowledge from another person as trustworthy, generalisable and relevant to the self. Epistemic trust is there to ensure that the individual can safely challenge and potentially change his way of thinking and feeling; it triggers the opening of an *epistemic superhighway* (Fonagy *et al.*, 2015), that is an evolutionarily protected mechanism that signals the individual's willingness to acquire knowledge.

In the best of circumstances when a patient and therapist have worked together in a shared space the patient has an experience of whether what the therapist says is of relevance to the problems he needs help with. Relevance results partly from the extent to which the therapist, drawing on the shared embodied experience in the consulting room, is attuned to the patient's embodied internal world and experience in the transference. Repeated exchanges with a therapist whose interventions are experienced as relevant builds up a store of trust that can compensate to a degree for the losses incurred when there is no access to embodied co-presence in a shared physical space. The greater the felt-to-be relevance, the greater the patient's epistemic trust and hence the greater the tolerance for the limitations and frustrations of mediated therapy. This, of course, assumes that patient and therapist have benefited from in-person sessions before transitioning to Skype.

In any mediated therapeutic encounter *epistemic vigilance* towards deception and misinformation is heightened. Relevance, we might say, relates to the truth-value of the therapist's interventions and hence the trust that the patient can place in the therapist. In mediated psychotherapy a crucial relational dynamic that reinforces or undermines the perceived relevance and corollary trust is the patient's experience that the therapist is telling the truth about the nature of the Skype therapy and how it impacts on the patient. In other words when working in a mediated therapeutic setting it is incumbent on the therapist that she communicates to the patient how this medium is experienced by him and how it intersects with the prerogatives of his internal world. The therapist thus facilitates the conditions for the relaxation of epistemic vigilance (i.e. the self-protective suspicion towards information coming from others that may be potentially damaging or deceptive) through the creation of an experience of feeling thought about (i.e. our experience and needs are anticipated) in relation to the mediated therapy the therapist is offering the patient.

If the patient's experience is not validated by the therapist, perhaps because the therapist believes that Skype therapy and in-person therapy are functionally equivalent, or because the therapist is not attuned to the patient's unconscious experience of Skype, then the risk is that the therapist's interventions will not be experienced as relevant to the patient and the therapeutic process becomes corrupted. Instead of being experienced as genuine attempts to arrive at the patient's truth about his experience the therapist's interventions are experienced as lies.

I will now illustrate through my work with Martin why when working via Skype it is important to listen to the patient's experience of this medium and to articulate its implications for how the therapist is experienced by the patient.

Martin

Martin was one of the first patients with whom I used Skype in the context of an ongoing in-person therapy three times weekly on the couch. When his job changed and demanded regular travel such that his three sessions were frequently at risk, he asked if we could make up the sessions by Skype. After much consideration, and given how committed he was to his therapy, we decided that it would be worth trying to use Skype so that he would not miss too many sessions.

Martin's original reason for seeking therapy was his unhappy marriage to a woman who though kind and supportive of him experienced significant inhibitions around her sexuality. Martin was also very troubled by his own sexuality that he struggled to integrate into a loving relationship. We had come to understand how he had 'chosen' his wife because he knew that her difficulties would ensure protection against his own profound anxieties about being sexual and emotionally intimate. He felt his wife was a reliable companion on whom he could 'download' his work worries and discuss the children but the relationship nevertheless felt 'dead'.

Now that their children were older and had left home, Martin was aware of emptiness in the marriage and he was concerned about his split off sexuality. He frequented prostitutes and while at first this had felt very exciting he was increasingly left feeling that this activity was 'dirty' and dangerous because he feared being exposed at work.

When we started using Skype the first thing that became clear was not only that we were not meeting in the same shared physical space, but also that due to being in different time zones, even if the session time was set at the usual UK time, Martin was not actually having his session at the same time as me. Similarly, although I was still in the same consulting room where we met physically when he called, he was in a distinctly different physical space, typically his hotel room or office and both varied.

We had discussed the importance of finding a private space free from intrusions but this proved difficult and sometimes served his own need to be interrupted: his office space could never feel entirely safe and private. He also inhabited the space differently: he was not my patient on a couch and I was not sitting behind him listening. At work he was his professional self, sitting opposite a computer screen and this often contributed to exchanges between us that were interesting to him but that I thought approximated at best a kind of 'coaching' relationship. There is nothing wrong with coaching if that is what the patient seeks. But if the patient has committed to an analytic process then it is the therapist's responsibility to provide this.

After two Skype sessions I noticed the impoverishment of our dialogue: it all felt rather superficial and I struggled to remain connected to him. Martin seemed cut off from this change and consciously reported finding the Skype sessions helpful. What I could see of his upper body recounted a different story. Martin was leaning away from the screen as if he wanted to interpose more distance between us. His arms were crossed and he was rocking in the chair. I recalled that when on the couch he seemed more relaxed and less agitated. The comparison I could make between what I had experienced with him physically present in the room with me is one of several types of information that I could draw on to make sense of what was transpiring between us virtually. Had I never shared a physical space with him, this would not have been accessible to me.

I invited Martin to reflect on how different he was and how I seemed to have become like his wife: a companion he 'downloaded' on but the exchange between us was emotionally distant, dead. Martin responded with silence and then reported a dream that he had the night before the second Skype session:

> *I am in a deserted bar and I am drinking pint after pint of beer. Strangely I don't feel drunk but when I get up from the bar stool I can barely stand up. I fall over and I am unconscious. I wake up days later and my body is in a state of decay.*

Martin associated to the dream and told me that when he was travelling he got into bad habits like going to sleep late, watching Internet pornography and drinking more than he should. He was troubled by his use of pornography, the 'compelling yet cheap images of sex', as he put it, that he downloaded on his screen. He thought that perhaps this was his way of also rebelling against the mundane routines he abided by when at home with his wife such that when he was away he could 'let rip' and indulge in excess. He recognised that it left him feeling bad about himself.

We eventually understood this dream as directly connected with the change to our setting: despite the continuity in the sessions and how grateful he was consciously for my willingness to adapt to his needs, unconsciously there was a very different narrative. Martin actually felt that by agreeing to Skype I had 'deserted' him. The computer screen that he watched pornography on and that left him feeling at the mercy of 'cheap images' was the same as the one on which my image appeared. This seemed to provide a powerful metaphor for how degraded the analytic process had become. Once we were able to acknowledge this the session became more alive and seemed to approximate our in-person sessions.

On another occasion, some weeks later, Martin had the session from his hotel room. He acknowledged that it seemed strange to speak to me from his 'bedroom' but that he felt this was not a problem. I was less than persuaded by this, but since I was then still relatively inexperienced with Skype, I was stymied and at first said nothing. As the session progressed, however, I grew increasingly uncomfortable about the quality of the exchanges between us: Martin's manner was unusually flirtatious as he laughed off how strange it would be if the hotel cleaner walked in and overheard him talking to me about his sexual problems.

I was mindful of the complex issues around confidentiality that need to be borne in mind when we work with Skype, represented here by the third-party figure of the cleaner in his associations. I was clear that Martin did not feel safe but interestingly this anxiety was here managed through sexualisation: we were now in his bedroom essentially having a threesome. This was exciting to him but it was clearly not therapy and just like he felt bad about himself downloading porn, I sensed that our corrupted exchange did not actually feel help-ful. The use of Skype had turned the consulting room into a bedroom and I had colluded with this.

Once interpreted this dynamic was helpful and re-established the frame of the therapy as Martin was relieved that I recognised what I had enabled by agreeing to Skype therapy and how he then used it to enact a familiar dynamic. Re-establishing this reality, and taking my share of responsibility for colluding with this, allowed us to consider the conditions under which Skype therapy could best operate for Martin. It reassured him that I was attuned to what he felt about Skype.

After a few months of intermittent Skype sessions we nevertheless reached the conclusion that it was better to miss sessions than to use Skype. This felt like a more truthful position in so far as it was attuned to Martin's idiosyncratic experience of Skype and how it primarily served his defensive needs. This might not be so for all patients, which is why it is the therapist's responsibility to carefully track any given patient's unconscious experience of mediated ther-apy, but it was so for Martin.

Tuning into the body

Psychoanalytic therapy that is carried out *exclusively* by Skype compromises many features of what it means to work psychoanalyti-cally such that, as some colleagues suggest, it begs the question of whether we can call it a psychoanalytic therapy at all. I am not saying that it cannot be helpful. That is an entirely separate question. But the setting is so altered that the therapist cannot reliably and effectively draw on the full range of competences required to work analytically, namely using the transference-countertransference matrix as the fundamental frame for understanding the unfolding of the patient's internal world (Lemma *et al.*, 2008). This matrix is embedded in implicit procedures of self-in-interaction-with-an-other that are often expressed by the patient and received by the therapist through their non-verbal exchanges. The loss of the embodied setting is a vital aspect of the analytic frame that is severely undermined through Skype and that deprives us of vital information.

Russell (2015) suggests that when we eliminate the experience of 'being bodies together' we constrain and limit what is therapeutically possible to 'states of mind' rather than 'states of being'. As a result, reflective introspection is undermined. She carefully and persuasively documents significant differences between Skype therapy and physically co-present therapy across a variety of therapeutic processes such as providing a facilitating, holding environment, adopting a stance of evenly suspended attention or developing conditions for shared reverie.

When the therapist works through virtually embodied presence she is deprived of the full range of her *somatic countertransference* to orient herself in relation to the patient's unconscious communications. The therapist's capacity to tune into the 'body wavelength' (Pugh, 2016) is severely curtailed. This is a significant loss with all patients. It is especially so with those patients who have difficulty in establishing and maintaining a stable differentiation from the object and who typically present with marked difficulties in symbolisation and may therefore powerfully project into the analyst's body. These patients, in my experience, are not suited to mediated therapy.

The analyst's somatic reactions may be understood to result from projective processes that bypass verbal articulation and that are deposited in the body, as it were. The patient's 'bodily states of mind' (Wyre, 1997) inevitably impact on and are impacted on by the analyst's bodily states of mind: the patient communicates through his body and the analyst receives such communications in their body. Such bodily experiences need to become 'thoughts with a thinker', to play on Bion's (1967) turn of phrase, and eventually shared with the patient in order to support the development of a capacity to symbolise. However with some patients the analyst's 'sensory acceptance' (Lombardi and Pola, 2010) of the patient's projections may be an essential prerequisite before interpretations can be helpful – this is nigh impossible on Skype.

Despite the significant limitations placed on the therapist's capacity to use the somatic countertransference I have also experienced moving developments in my work with patients via Skype. How can we understand this? In order to make sense of positive outcomes there are two closely connected issues that need to be considered beyond the question of relevance that was discussed earlier.

First, when therapist and patient have a history of working together in the same physical space prior to transitioning to Skype (permanently or intermittently) then the therapist can draw on this prior shared embodied experience. This allows her to use embodied and affectively charged *somatic markers* to reconnect with the patient despite the virtual working conditions. Such markers are polysemic and can cross-reference to multi-layered transference experiences encountered in the in-person setting. They can be very powerful and help to viscerally ground both patient and therapist despite the virtual space in which they meet when on Skype. For example, the therapist can reference when working virtually the past *in situ* experience of the patient's use of the consulting room, of his posture, of his breathing. This can help to reconnect the patient to a shared historical understanding of his internal world gleaned from these somatic manifestations.

Memories of our experiences are likely characterised by representations in the form of neuronal activity. Activity among a network of neurons represents a code for the experience of, say, 'when my therapist understood why I get anxious'. When this network is activated by some cue that triggers a re-experience of that intersubjective event, we have recollected that experience. I am suggesting here that the somatic marker acts as such a cue, as I will illustrate shortly through my work with Mala.

Second, because the shared embodied experience *in situ*, at its best, allows the therapist to understand the patient's non-verbally expressed internal world with greater specificity and accuracy, the somatic markers drawn from shared in-person experience re-evoke, and in turn reinforce, the perceived relevance by the patient of what the therapist offers in the virtual setting. In other words the memory of the in-person experience via the somatic marker reconnects the patient to an experience of feeling known and understood by the therapist in a unique way specific to this particular relationship. This deepens the felt emotional bond between patient and therapist through the use the therapist makes of the memory in order to understand the patient, hence it increases perceived relevance.

The virtual setting and the Skype medium that makes this connection possible can be experienced as the 'uncanny third' (Dettbarn, 2013). Somatic markers, however, offset or relax the epistemic vigilance mobilised by the virtual setting.

Mala

Mala, a successful business woman in her thirties, was posted abroad after 18 months of working with me three times weekly on the couch. The comparatively small country she was relocating to had CBT therapists and some psychodynamic counsellors but no one who was fully analytically trained. After much discussion we decided that it was better, on balance, for us to continue working together via Skype with an understanding that she would visit London three times per year for two weeks and have in-person sessions during those six weeks each year.

Before sharing some of our Skype exchanges I want to give a flavour of the in-person experience. Mala had originally sought help because of a very difficult relationship with her mother whom she had experienced as intrusive into her body and mind. She spent the first nine months of the therapy enveloped in long periods of silence that I felt were intended to keep me at a distance and to protect herself from my anticipated intrusion.

Because Mala said very little my interventions were often based on my somatic countertransference. As Mala walked in and out of my room she would keep her head bowed low as she shook my hand. The hand-shaking, which was culturally consistent with Mala's background, exposed me to her invariably sweaty palms. Curiously when we shook hands the very first time – and this made a lasting impression – I had the association that she was wiping her sweat on me as if to penetrate me. I had experienced a strong urge at the time to wash my hands.

During the many months when I sat behind the couch waiting for Mala to speak I reflected on this paradoxical visceral experience: on the one hand it felt as if Mala seeped into my skin through her sweaty palms and this felt intrusive; on the other hand, Mala shut me out of her mind through her impregnable silence. The only movement, as it were, came from the way she flexed her left foot backwards and forwards for extended periods of time, always in the same direction, as she lay otherwise very still on the couch. This had an autoerotic quality that had an unsurprisingly distancing effect on me.

I was often sleepy during sessions. My mind wandered easily as she could spend 40 minutes in total silence, not even responding to my attempts to engage with her. I was thus penetrated and shut out with equal force.

A few months into our work Mala lay on the couch and suddenly got up panic stricken. She turned round apologetically and explained that she was worried that she might have stained my couch because she had just 'come on', as she put it. She checked the cover on the couch for stains and then relaxed as she said that it had been a 'false alarm'. Once again in the supine position she told me that her mind was blank. I observed that her mind a few minutes earlier has been filled with panic and alarm at the thought that she might have left a bloody stain on my cover. Mala was silent for a long while and then said that the thought horrified her, that if she had stained the cover she would have struggled to come back such would have been her shame. She thought she could now smell an unpleasant odour and she feared it was coming from her body and that I would think it repulsive.

As I listened I was mindful that her sweaty hands and now the fantasy of her menstrual blood staining my cover and her body odour were powerful visceral ways in which she leaked into my space/body. I thought that her fear that she might have 'come on' was a displaced reference to her longing to 'come on' to me and be sexually intimate with me. But her erotic longing elicited a toxic mixture of excitement, anxiety and shame.

Through my descriptions of Mala's body and physical experience as she related to the setting of my consulting room I have illustrated how the primary source of communication and information that I had to work from for some months was primarily sensory in nature (visual, olfactory, tactile and kinaesthetic). This type of interaction could never be observed and processed by a therapist in a mediated therapy with the exception of some very limited visual information. Yet, over time, in the in-person setting these somatic reactions and the associations they elicited in me allowed us to make some sense of Mala's most likely pre-verbal experience with her mother, a woman who had suffered several severe psychotic breakdowns. She alternated between periods when she was very high and intrusive into Mala's body and periods of severe depression when she became completely inaccessible to Mala.

The transition to Skype therapy was not easy, not least because Mala was deeply unsettled by the move as her mother had also recently died. She felt she had lost all moorings. Mala tried to replicate as much of the original therapy consulting room setting in the new country by creating a private space in her flat with a couch. She would lie on the couch with the iPad next to her head (out of her sight but within ear reach). We Skyped without the visual function activated except to say hello and goodbye largely because the use of the visual function led to frequent technical breakdowns that interrupted the session.

As we worked through the Skype medium I was conscious that I needed to work very hard to represent her in my mind, for example to imagine her lying on my couch and recall the bodily movements that I had grown so accustomed to. When I rooted myself back in my somatic memory of her I felt more attuned. This was not just an internal process. I frequently also checked with Mala how she was feeling (more so than I would do in an in-person setting) and tried to encourage her to describe her bodily experience to me so as to root *her* in her bodily experience.

Where appropriate I would draw on familiar somatic markers. For example, by the time we transitioned to Skype we had openly discussed her sweaty hands and how exposed she felt when she shook my hand as it betrayed her anxiety about being received by me 'warts and all'. We also understood a bit more about her wish to leak into me. On one occasion, when discussing via Skype an incident that pointed to her own intrusiveness, I 'marked' my intervention with a reference to the somatic expression of both anxiety and intrusiveness that we had experienced in person when we shook hands.

Mala's response to this 'marker' was of note: she became quite tearful and then made reference to how she missed my room and its distinctive smell. She told me that she had recently searched for a candle that smelt like my room. She had felt low as she shopped as she could not find anything that approximated this and she wished I would tell her the brand of candle that burned in my room.

We were able to then reflect together on how as soon as she recalled our hand-shaking she was back in my room and she wanted to recreate it where she was now located. I said that I thought she was asking me to offer her the 'brand' of therapy that is rooted in real smells, not its virtual adaptation. Mala was relieved to hear me say this, she replied.

Unlike Martin, it seemed possible to continue with Skype with Mala, not least because she had permanently relocated so that the options were even worse by comparison. In my work with Mala it was important to acknowledge the loss that our virtual work carried and that despite her gratitude for being able to continue our work together, she recognised that it was not the same. Crucially she needed me to recognise this too, as I discussed earlier in relation to Martin.

The slippery slope of Skype

The analytic relationship unfolds in the context of a paradox that defines the analytic setting: it is a relationship that relies on the establishment of mutuality in the context of a vital asymmetry (Aron, 1996; Celenza, 2010). The commitment made by patient and therapist to work together holds out the hope for and promise of continued acceptance and understanding for the patient of even the most hated aspects of the self. This is a powerful interpersonal experience that taps into a universal longing to be loved 'warts and all' without the requirement to give anything back to the one who loves us.

It can be said that the treatment setting both stimulates and frustrates these universal wishes. Moreover this peculiar mix intensifies the experience and longing for intimacy and mobilises erotic longings in the psychoanalytic dyad. Indeed the analytic setting is stimulating, seductive and frustrating for the therapist too. The analytic contract is defined by the asymmetric distribution of attention paid to the patient by the therapist. The requirement of the therapist to dismiss personal need is frustrating and depleting. This deprivation sets the scene, as it were, for how the therapist may therefore be partially 'gratified and titillated' by the moments of attunement that the patient offers:

It might be said that *the frustration of asymmetry is counterbalanced by the seduction of mutuality and momentary attunements; 'we're in this together differently' mistakenly becoming 'we're in this together the same.'* These vicarious identifications evoke and temporarily unsettle the analyst as he or she decenters and resonates with the analysand's experience. (Celenza, 2010: 64, original italics)

Psychoanalytic therapy thus takes place within the highly seductive context of therapeutic asymmetry. This contemporaneously depleting and seductive structure means that the therapist needs both professional consultation and a stable setting in which to maintain or re-establish equilibrium. The embodied setting is an important anchor in this respect: it contains the therapist as much as the patient.

A significant risk posed by new technologies in the context of a therapeutic process is that they are seductively informal such that the therapist can all too easily find herself on the *slippery slope of Skype*. The so-called slippage arises partly because Skype engenders a relaxation of the boundaries of the setting. Indeed, sometimes the very notion of 'setting' becomes increasingly loose. For example, it is not uncommon for patients to use Skype via their cell phones and carry out their session in the most unlikely of places (a park, a taxi). Likewise for therapists: they may start to offer Skype sessions from locations other than their own office. I have done this too on one occasion, rationalised in terms of 'keeping continuity' when I was working abroad, only to quickly learn why I would never do so again when I found myself struggling to adjust the screen to avoid any evidence of the bed in my hotel room. It was a disturbing and sobering experience that helped me to realise how I had lost sight of the setting and had been drawn into an enactment.

Different media are experienced on a continuum from formal to informal with a spectrum of legitimations and rationalisations of what each medium adds to the person's idiosyncratic mix of unconscious association within personal communication. The portable nature of various media is an important feature since the laptop used for Skype therapy may be the same one used for downloading pornography, for example. Where the media is used may also be relevant: Skype when sitting at a desk may be felt to be formal but not when using a smartphone in a hotel room, for example. Importantly such media encourage a kind of chummy friendliness or casualness that is typically more reigned in when working in-person. This creates a context ripe for enactments on both sides.

We do well to remember, as Freud (1919) emphasised, the importance of abstinence in our work. He proposed that once the therapist becomes an important object to the patient, that is once she becomes invested as the target of transference wishes, the therapist should leave these wishes ungratified and instead analyse the defences that develop. Clinical experience repeatedly demonstrates that affect soon emerges in response to the experience of frustration along with the accompanying phantasies that are elicited and the defences to manage this. This allows the therapist to help the patient examine his conflicts. In other words, abstinence gives rise to a state of deprivation crucial to treatment.

As I suggested in Chapter 3 we now live and work in a world where a 'state of deprivation' has little currency, if any at all: desiring, waiting and frustrations are encumbrances rather than states of mind that bear their fruit when tolerated. This shapes the expectation patients have of therapy and that therapists can sometimes also share: that therapy should be provided no matter what or where, when needed. Like anonymity, that optimal state of deprivation that Freud regarded as crucial to treatment is undermined in our current practice. Mediated therapy can be experienced as deeply gratifying. It can feed into fantasies of greater intimacy and of ease of access to the therapist. These may be left unexplored because the use of the virtual medium can be all too easily rationalised in a world where mediation is the order of the day.

It is not only because the setting is potentially felt to be more 'relaxed' and in some respects more gratifying that it is more possible to slip into enactments when working through the virtual medium. The absence of the two bodies in a shared physical space also plays an important part. Some argue that a virtual relationship protects the patient who may be anxious about sexual or aggressive transgressions by the other. Paradoxically, however, it is precisely because of the physical proscription imposed by the fact of mediation that problems arise. When the actual bodies are not directly implicated, the relationship that unfolds in a virtual space can more readily become seductive: the fact that 'nothing can happen *really*' (i.e. 'I am in love with my therapist but we can never consummate the relationship because we are not in the same room') seduces both patient and therapist away from reflecting on what *is* nevertheless happening between them at the level of fantasy. The frame of a physically co-present context is vital, I am suggesting, for protecting patient and therapist from the slippery slope of Skype. When both bodies share the same space the somatic countertransference can be more easily noted and relied upon with greater confidence and this can minimise enactments.

Suler (2004) has written about the 'online disinhibition effect' that is characterised by the following: dissociative anonymity (what I do cannot be traced back to me); invisibility (no one can see what I look like); asynchronicity (my actions do not occur in real time); solipsistic introjection (I can't see the other(s) so I have to guess who they are and their intent); dissociative imagination (these are not real people); minimisation of authority (I can act freely). Several of these features are not relevant to Skype therapy because it is a visual medium where both participants are known to each other. However, the last two features, 'dissociative imagination' and 'minimisation of authority', pose risks precisely because virtual communication does not require our embodied presence in the same space as that of the patient: as the body becomes unmoored it can precipitate action rather than reflection.

Indeed it could be argued that erotic excitement – a normal and expectable response in an analytic dyad – can function as an alert by locating our experience in our bodies. When such excitement occurs through mediation, where the body of the other and one's own can be dismissed and the whole experience can be written off as 'virtual' and hence not real, the risk of transgression can be minimised and the therapist may consequently be less attuned to it. The danger is that the virtual meeting encourages a 'pretend' state of mind (Fonagy and Target, 1996) in both participants where the mental world is decoupled from external reality. And yet even if the therapist and patient do not physically act on each other's bodies they can still act powerfully on each other's minds with detrimental consequences for the patient if the therapist does not remain watchful of the transference-countertransference. Co-presence stands a better chance of helping the therapist to identify and analyse physical sensations that protect against acting out on loving and erotic longings in particular.

The technological medium thus acts in one (limited) sense as a protective physical shield since the therapist or the patient cannot actually touch each other, but psychically the technological medium can precipitate simultaneously disinhibition and minimisation with respect to erotic longings that when left unchecked pervert the course of therapy. The evidence for this is often subtle and defences are typically mobilised against conscious awareness of this in the therapist and patient. Yet the patient's unconscious narrative tells a very different story, as I will illustrate in the following brief clinical vignette of a case I supervised. I should add that the therapist was an experienced clinician, trained as a psychodynamic therapist, who learnt a great deal through this case – as did I – as she was very inexperienced with Skype.

John

Dr B., a female therapist, had been working once weekly with John, face-to-face, for about six months before he was promoted and had to relocate abroad. He had originally sought help following his separation from his wife and the acceptance of this new job coincided with his painful realisation that the marriage was irretrievable.

During the first few weeks of Skype therapy John expressed his gratitude to Dr B. for continuing to work with him. He said that he felt lonely and dislocated in the new country. Dr B. was quick and correct to observe that the Skype medium left him feeling dislocated from her and John reassured her that this was a lifeline for him irrespective of the limitations.

Dr B. felt very identified with John's sense of loss because she had also recently divorced. She was aware of the risk this posed and was able to reflect on it with me in supervision. However, I noted that since John had moved abroad and they communicated via Skype, Dr B. seemed keen to emphasise to me his urgent need for support and attunement. She agreed to change his session time twice without any exploration of what this might mean, which struck me as somewhat at odds with how careful she was typically. Then she reported to me that John had texted her on his way to work because he had felt anxious and needed to feel connected to her and she had replied with some reassuring words. Dr B. acknowledged that this was 'unusual' but she also felt that John was very alone and needed to draw on her support. I sensed that she was too quick to explain instead of being curious about what this might mean. It seemed as though the greater the physical distance between them the more inclined she was to narrow the field of her analytic vision.

I encouraged her to explore with him this 'unusual' behaviour in their next session, from which I have permission to share the following brief excerpt:

J: Thank you for replying to my text … it really helped me to get through the day … I am struggling right now and I feel you are the only person who knows me … I am surrounded by strangers or work colleagues …feels quite lonely …

T: You don't feel seen ... recognised for who you are ...

J: Yes, that's exactly right ... it's like I'm invisible ... I have no roots here, and it feels so strange to say that I'm separated when people ask me about my wife ... I called my mother last night, tried to Face Time her but she is hopeless with this technology (laughs) and so she said I should just use the telephone ...

T: You felt rejected by her suggestion of the phone instead of actually seeing you ...

J: Well, you know, it's nice to have some more substantial connection ... like now ... I mean seeing you on Skype at least makes it more real ... I had this urge today to be held ... I thought I might even pay for sex just so as to be held ... but then I remembered that we had a session and I thought this was more important ...

T: More real ...

J: Yes, because I know that you care about me ... that text I sent you ... I really thought you would not reply ... I thought I might have overstepped the mark but when you did ... just the few words you wrote made me feel better ...

T: You didn't trust that I would respond to your pain ... you anticipated rejection like with your mother who did not want to use Face Time ...

   (Silence)

J: I dreamt last night that I had gone to my meeting with my old boss and he was behaving strangely. I kept thinking that it was not him, but some kind of impostor ... he looked familiar but I was not comfortable. He offered me a new job in Asia and said I would be a fool to turn it down. I really don't like Asia, but he said he would move there too and I could work with him and we could make lots of money.

I will not go further into this session but I would like to draw attention to a few aspects pertinent to this discussion.

Prior to the session John texts his therapist in a manner that suggests he is relating to her more as if she was a friend or lover. In fact he tells her that he was not expecting her to reply (i.e. he recognises that he has crossed a boundary) but when Dr B. replies she gratifies his longing to be close to her and to find his surrogate partner in her. Instead of taking this up in the session, as we had agreed in supervision, and reflecting on her own enactment, Dr B. instead plays on the register of attunement and focuses on how John does not feel seen by the other: on what he is missing that she instead now provides. This arouses John who then tells Dr B. how he longs to be touched and how he almost went to see a prostitute but then recalled that he had his Skype session with Dr B. Here we can see the beginning of John's unconscious representation of his therapist: she is equated with a prostitute: someone who gets paid to provide sexual comfort.

Dr B.'s response is not to take up either the perversion of the analytic setting that she has contributed to or the erotic longing in the transference. Instead she links her response to how John felt rejected by the mother who, as it happens, stands as the figure who will *not* use a virtual medium. Dr B. responds very seductively by reinforcing that his encounter with her was 'more real' – though paradoxically this encounter is in fact virtual. This leads John to elaborate further the seductive dance when he says: 'I know that you care about me.'

Through his dream John, however, is beginning to represent unconsciously the meaning of the gratifying exchange and to communicate this to Dr B. In this dream John meets his boss – a familiar figure with whom in theory he has an asymmetric relationship – who is now, however, behaving 'strangely' and invites him to go to Asia with him but where John does not really want to go (i.e. the therapist has agreed to work with him in another virtual setting/country which is not the setting that John wants to work in). We might say that Dr B., like the boss in the dream who entices him with the lure of money, is experienced as seductive. The dream thus vividly encapsulates John's experience of not actually recognising his 'old' therapist in this new Skype setting turning her into some kind of 'impostor'.

The peculiarity of the analytic setting with all its conventions might be odd and frustrating at times, but it does at least ensure that the boundaries of the analytic relationship are clearly demarcated as different to a social relationship. As such any longings for attachment or erotic feelings that either party might have are more reliably constrained by the setting that serves here as a reminder that the analytic relationship is different to any other kind of intimate relationship even when it gives rise to familiar and compelling feelings.

Concluding thoughts

We can think of 'place' as fixity, for example a location on a map or where our consulting room is, in relation to 'space' as 'a practiced place' (De Certeau, 1984: 117). A street, for example, is transformed into 'space' by walkers. A room in a physical and virtual location is transformed into the 'analytic space' by patient and therapist and the contract that binds them together for the 50 minutes in that space. Therefore places come into being by people engaged in a given activity. Places are 'constantly being performed '(Creswell, 2004: 37). Rethinking place as performed and prac-tised in radically open ways provides another means of investigating the embodied experience of therapy in an actual consulting room versus in a virtual place. Place in this sense becomes an event marked by the quality of the communication between two people rather than the boundedness or permanence of the actual space of meeting with the attendant advantages and limitations that pertain to the absence of the bounded space of the actual consulting room. The latter may be more or less important depend-ing on the psychic state of the patient. As such the question of whether mediated therapy is 'good' or 'bad' really needs to be a question about whether it works or not for a specific patient–therapist dyad that practise psychoanalysis together.

As I have explored in this chapter there are significant challenges to mediated therapy. The ever-present question in my mind is whether it would be more honest to refuse to do Skype therapy given the losses and risks that I have outlined. Based on my experience I am of the view that analytic therapy offered via Skype is always the poor relation of the actual in-person experience. We cannot replicate a fully shared embodied experi-ence in virtual space: at best we can approximate to it and compensate for what is lost when we are not in shared physical space. It is vital to know this with integrity and base decisions about Skype therapy with this knowledge in mind. Being truthful is always important in our work. Truthfulness relates to a state of mind towards the other and not only to a statement of fact. Being truthful is about intentionality and, as such, lies at the core of the patient's experience with his therapist: it determines whether the patient can trust her intentions towards him.

The question of the trustworthiness of the sources of information has become more prescient today because we live in what has been aptly termed a 'post-truth' world (Pomerantsev, 2016). It is not only that we are fed lies by politicians through various media outlets, for example, but also, and even more corrosive, is the fact that lying itself is seemingly not considered to be a problem. This is the context that made it possible for British politicians to stage a Brexit campaign in 2016 with promises such as 'Let's give our NHS the £350 million the EU takes every week' but, on winning the referendum, the claim was dismissed as a 'mistake' by one Brexit leader while another dismissed it as no more than 'an aspiration'.

Does technology exert an influence on our relationship to truth? I am of the view that it does. There are two reasons for this. First, new media with its many screens and streams of information allow us to escape into virtual realities and fantasies where the felt-to-be truth of one's internal world is isomorphic with external reality and impervious to any other version of reality. Second, there is increasing awareness that the so-called information age allows lies to spread very rapidly. The sheer volume of 'disinformation cascades' makes it hard to distinguish truth from lies (Pomerantsev, 2016). All that matters is that the lie is clickable, and what determines that is how it feeds into people's existing prejudices. Google and Facebook have developed algorithms that are based around our previous searches and clicks: with every search and every click we find our own biases confirmed, feeding us only the things that make us feel better, irrespective of whether they are true or not. We are being manipulated on a daily basis and we are unaware of how complicit we are in this process since we are suppliers of the personal data that make the manipulation possible in the first place.

In an external climate where truth is thus debased, lying is of no consequence and where it supports self-confirmatory biases, the provision of psychotherapy through the same media that promulgate lies requires careful consideration. As Churcher (2015) has compellingly argued privacy, for example, cannot be safeguarded via Skype. If we extol the fundamental importance of confidentiality and then work through a medium that cannot protect it what are we actually communicating to our patients? We are fudging the truth. The only way to restore integrity is to keep open a dialogue with the patient about what is lost or compromised through this medium for working therapeutically instead of relating to Skype as if it were no more than the next 'new' adaptation of how we work, something that we merely have to take in our stride.

On balance, and given the culture we now operate in, I have decided that I need to engage with this medium but to do so only on certain conditions:

1   It is important to meet the patient in person several times before embarking on Skype and ideally to have worked with them in person over a more extended period before transitioning to Skype.

2   It is essential to be explicit with the patient about the limitations of Skype and to assiduously listen for what this unconsciously means and interpret this.

3   Patients have to be carefully selected for this medium. Unsuitable for this medium are patients who have body image disturbances, those who are borderline and/or perverse, those with limited capacity to represent experience, those who experience difficulty with differentiating from the other and those whose grasp on reality is tenuous. What these patients have in common is a need to be rooted in their own bodies as they relate to the embodied setting provided by the therapist's actual presence in order to work through their conflicts.

4   It is important to be firm with those patients whose needs would not be met by working in this way even if this means turning away work.

5   This way of working requires that the therapist carefully monitors her behaviour when using Skype because it is a much harder medium that deprives the therapist of access to her somatic countertransference and hence, counter-intuitively, there are greater risks of erotic enactments via this medium.

Notes

1   I am using the terms setting and frame interchangeably.

2   Riva and Mantovani (2014) outline three features of presence: it locates the self in an external physical and cultural space, it provides feedback to the self about the status of its activity and it allows for the evolution of the self through the incorporation of tools. They also outline three levels of presence – *proto*, *core* and *extended presence* – with the most evolutionary superior being extended presence. The latter is defined as the 'intuitive perception of successfully acting in the external world towards a possible object'.

Chapter 5

Digital transference and the therapist's anonymity

Stan

A man in his fifties, Stan was made redundant after a very successful career. A year on he had become depressed: he did not need money as he had ample savings set aside, but he now felt aimless and his marriage was 'stale'. Soon his twice-weekly sessions with me became the centre-piece of his week. He had not yet told his wife that he was receiving therapy because he feared that she would disapprove as she was against therapy. Yet I sensed that the secret served a more important psychic function for Stan: it created excitement as if he and I were having an affair. As such it became a powerful antidote to his depression and the staleness in his marriage that he was afraid to confront.

Some months into the therapy Stan 'confessed' to me, as he put it, that he had been Googling me and complimented me on the range of my work. He said that it had given him a 'window into' the kind of person I was and that this had been reassuring to him: he had felt that he was in safe hands. He told me that he had managed to find my date of birth and had been impressed by what I had achieved quite young. He liked the fact that I was a successful professional woman. He hoped that I would not mind, that he had not intended to be intrusive. As he spoke I was aware of his appropriation of me.

As we eventually understood it, Stan's Internet search was not an isolated incident but a regular feature of how he nourished his 'secret' relationship with me and derived gratification from it. The 'data' that Stan obtained about me, to which he had finally 'confessed', supported a fantasy of intimacy with me and ownership of me: in this part of his mind he appropriated my so-called success and entertained a gratifying fantasy that we were a successful couple working together. This fantasy was narcissistically and sexually gratifying.

When I began practising as a clinician thirty years ago none of my patients could have found out my age or got hold of my CV as Stan was able to do with relative ease. If you grew up before mobiles and social networking were the norm you will only recall George Orwell's dystopian, all-seeing Big Brother as a character in a novel who eradicated the possibility of any private life or unspoken thoughts. Nowadays, however, this character is an all too eerily accurate description of the twentieth-century way of being: one characterised by the presence of technologies that have turned us into data. As data we can be accessed freely, tracked and used by ourselves as much as by others for pragmatic and psychological ends.

Practically everyone's lives are accessible and offered for display resulting also in a newly pervasive, permeable and transient sense of self in which what we experience and feel has migrated to the phone, to the digital cloud and to the shape-shifting judgement of others through social media.

Advances in information communication technology are dramatically improving real-time communication and information-sharing. By improving access to information and facilitating global debate, they foster democratic participation. But at the same time it has become clear that these new technologies are vulnerable to electronic surveillance and interception[1] (Churcher, 2015) and to misuse, for example through cyberbullying and stalking online.

On the one hand, a public culture of openness and transparency seems a necessary good. On the other hand, most who can still remember an era before intimate telephone conversations were broadcast on streets and trains feel more than bewildered by just how many of our private parts are publicly paraded. Cohen (2013) writes about the unholy 'alliance between voyeurism and exhibitionism' that marks our epoch's recalibration of the private. Our need to know, to probe secrets, he argues, is much more than an extension of a child's curiosity. Rather he suggests that the lure of exposure reflects a wish that nothing should remain unknown to us. He recognises that the emphasis on needing to know everything about the other mirrors the suspicion that there is always something we don't know – an unknown other who is also uncannily familiar, the bits that are too scary to acknowledge. Our epoch's frenzied attack on privacy may well be an attack on that all-too-human complexity that totalitarian states also seek to abolish (ffyche and Pick, 2016). That technology can fuel a totalitarian state of mind is borne out in my clinical experience.

In this chapter I will focus exclusively on the fate of the analyst's anonymity in contemporary times and its impact on the transference specifically. Clearly the question of our privacy is not something that we have any more control over as analysts than as citizens. Whatever our professional beliefs about the importance of anonymity for the analytic process we cannot in any way limit our patients' access to information about us that can be found on search engines, especially for those clinicians who are also involved in academic and other public pursuits and who therefore leave many digital footprints, but this affects all therapists to varying degrees. I will argue that for the more disturbed patients this easy, immediate access to information about the therapist, thereby bypassing the anonymity of the therapist that psychoanalysis has regarded as so vital to the analytic relationship, can precipitate severe forms of acting out. I will also consider, however, the way in which for some patients 'data' can be understood as a very modern type of 'transitional object' and I will argue that this use of data lends itself more readily to being analysed.

On anonymity and curiosity

Taken together the first descriptions of the analytic stance could be thought of as comprising a set of guidelines whose primary aim was to restrict the patient's awareness of the therapist as a real person thereby allowing the transference to develop unimpeded. This required the therapist to inhibit, to an extent, her so-called 'normal' personality and judgements so as to receive the patient's projections. Indeed Freud (1912) described how the therapist should function as a blank screen to the patient's projections so that the reactions to the therapist were likely to reflect a less contaminated picture of the patient's internal world. He thought that this required that the therapist follows the rule of abstinence and that her anonymity be preserved. Freud thus regarded any previous acquaintance with the patient or his relations as a serious disadvantage. He suggested that the therapist should not reveal to the patient her own emotional reactions or discuss her own experiences (Freud, 1913).

Even pre-Internet it was amply apparent that complete anonymity is impossible to sustain: those who make referrals to us may give something away about us to the patient and, in any event, the patient will almost certainly pick up a lot of clues about us. If nothing else our embodied nature ensures that we invariably communicate far more about who we are through our bodies than we like to think. Even where we strive to maintain as anonymous a stance as possible, for example by decorating neutrally our consulting rooms or by not seeing our patients within our own homes, patients will often be curious about us and draw conclusions about our person – sometimes from the most improbable sources. More often than not their assessments will contain at least some element of truth.

Pre-Internet, however, the therapist at least could make use of *relative* anonymity to examine the patient's conscious and unconscious fantasies about her as they emerged spontaneously over the course of an analysis or psychotherapy. This invariably generates a lot of meaningful material. Many patients are explicitly curious about their therapists. Behind such curiosity we often find unconscious motivations or wishes that deserve exploration. It is also of equal interest when the patient displays no curiosity whatsoever, as lack of curiosity may be, for example, a defence against erotic feelings in the transference or rivalrous feelings about the therapist's phantasised other patients/children.

Many of us will have struggled with whether or not to answer personal questions about what we think or feel or other personal facts. By and large, the rule of thumb in psychoanalytic work is that no question is ever innocent and therefore our task is to interpret its unconscious meaning. Let me illustrate this with a clinical example from my practice in 2001 when the Internet capacity was far more limited and did not allow people to upload as much information as can be uploaded now. As such the question this particular patient asked could not have been answered by an Internet search that nowadays, with some perseverance, could reveal the answer to. I say this because this same question was posed by one of my patients in 2014 and through various searches this patient satisfied himself that he could answer it (and was accurate).

Karen

Karen was a thirty-year-old woman who had been in three-times-weekly psychotherapy with me for four years. Some months after the traumatic events of September 11, 2001, she arrived for her session clearly irritable. Everything I said was rebuffed. She remarked that we were going round in circles and she could not see the point of what I said to her. She complained that she had come into therapy to be able to have a relationship and she was still not succeeding in this. The night before a man she had started to date made it clear that he had no wish to pursue the relationship further. Karen was very hurt by this rejection and felt despondent about any future relationships.

In the session Karen went on to talk about the difficulties at work since the events of September 11 and the number of redundancies in her profession. She was worried that sooner or later her name would be called out and she would be left without a job. She sardonically said to me 'Without job and a man! You've done a good job. You must be pleased with yourself. I just don't know why I bother with therapy.' Karen then fell into silence. After a few minutes she said, in a softer, more childlike tone that she felt sorry for the Jewish people, that the attacks on the Twin Towers were fundamentally attacks on the Jews. She thought the Jewish people would have to retaliate. She then paused and added: 'I've been meaning to ask you for some time, are you Jewish?' I did not say anything and Karen added, 'I guessed you would not answer. I don't get it. Why will you never answer my questions?' Karen went on to criticise me for not answering. She then paused and added, 'But I suppose that if you are Jewish you must have been feeling quite bad.

Karen's personal question cannot be considered to be simple curiosity about the therapist she has been seeing for four years whose religious affiliation had never concerned her before this point. Answering her question directly is unlikely to be of any benefit to her: she does not need to know whether I am Jewish or not in order for her to get the most out of the therapy. However, understanding why after four years in therapy with me she thinks to ask me about my religious affiliations could help her at this particular juncture. I therefore decided to intervene but not to answer the question directly.

My intervention was informed by tracking the sequence of the material Karen had produced. Karen arrives for the session hurt and angry. She begins by complaining about the therapy and its uselessness and then lets me know that her partner has rejected her. She then expresses her concerns about being made redundant at work. This represents a consciously realistic preoccupation and is thematically related to her first story of being rejected/made redundant by her partner.

She follows this up with an attack on me: I have not helped her and she does not know why she bothers with therapy.

Tracking the sequence of the session and the various themes allowed me to formulate my first hypothesis, namely that Karen manages her painful feelings of rejection by projecting them into me: I become the useless therapist who is not worth bothering with and is going to get dumped. My thoughts then turn to the fact that Karen is overtly hostile towards me and I wonder what the anticipated consequence of being hostile might be for her. Again, following the sequence of her associations, and in particular her question to me about whether I am Jewish, is helpful in this respect. After her attack on therapy, Karen switches tack: she talks about the Jewish people probably wanting to retaliate against the attacks. She is thus introducing a preoccupation with how people manage an attack that is very personal (i.e. it is not a random attack but it is linked in her mind with the personal attribute of being Jewish). Karen lets me know that in her own mind such an attack could only provoke a counter-attack. She then asks her direct question: 'Are you Jewish?' In light of the preceding sequence of associations I hear this question as expressing Karen's anxiety about her own hostile attack towards me. This was a very personal attack and it is as if she is saying to me: 'I have attacked you and you are now going to retaliate.'

This interpretation allowed Karen to then talk about her anger towards her mother whom she felt had set a very bad example as she had 'given up' on relationships. Karen feared she would end up alone like her mother, depressed. However, she felt guilty for criticising her mother in this manner as she recognised that her mother had sacrificed a great deal for her, having relinquished her own career after Karen's father left her.

By not answering Karen's question directly, Karen was able to begin to explore a painful dynamic with her mother, highlighting her identification with a mother who had 'given up', her anger about this and her feeling about having somehow been the cause of her mother's depression. Her attacks on her mother, in turn, gave rise to considerable guilt. The experience of asking a question and the confrontation with the absence of an answer pushes the patient to symbolise (Etchegoyen, 1991).

The fate of the patient's curiosity today

Fast-forward now some 15 years and we enter a fundamentally altered working environment that relegates the importance of the therapist's anonymity to bygone times. We now practise in a context where no sooner are we given someone's name the instinct, for most people and especially for the younger generation, is to Google them or check them out on LinkedIn.

Most of the patients I see nowadays will have Googled me prior to our first consultation and consider this to be a very normal form of pre-engagement. This is now part of a common shared repertoire for how the current generation makes decisions about how to meet their needs whether it be which washing machine to buy right through to which therapist to consult. In fact it is its everydayness that marks this behaviour as hard to interpret in a first meeting at this juncture of the twenty-first century. Whether we like it or not therapy is now considered a 'service' and as 'providers' of this service prospective 'clients' feel it appropriate to check out our credentials through the mediums that are now available. Not doing so is ironically the behaviour that stands out nowadays. In other words in a world where exposure is the order of the day, it is 'not wanting to know' that becomes (even more) interesting.

The culture of surveillance that underpins the invasion of privacy all around us is not one that I personally welcome but I think it is nevertheless important to carefully consider the meaning of any given behaviour in its cultural and historical context before attributing intrapsychic meaning to it. If the boundaries between public and private are more fluid or altogether absent in contemporary culture we need to pause before we interpret the meaning of this behaviour in our patients, especially the younger generation who have grown up in these times.

Of course we can always wonder with the patient about how anxious he felt about meeting us for the first time and how gaining some information prior to this meeting might be an attempt to manage this anxiety. However, I must confess that when I have made such interpretations in early sessions and specifically linked them to the patient's use of Google I have been less than convinced myself about their usefulness in most instances.

However, even if we accept that Googling one's prospective therapist is now commonplace, using Google and other social media to track the activities of one's analyst or to find out about private personal details remains, in my view, a behaviour that must be analysed. In this new technological context childish curiosity about what goes on in the parental/ analyst's bedroom can quickly escalate into a perverse intrusion into it and, if unexamined, can undermine the analytic process, on occasions making it unviable.

Internet stalking is commonplace and is not just restricted to following the off-screen lives of film or rock stars. Any patient who has access to the Internet can now have unprecedented access to their therapist's life beyond the couch. Online publication of written materials, YouTube videos of lectures, search engines that can easily reveal personal information from address to marital status to how much the analyst paid for their house have put paid to any notion of anonymity. When I now cancel a session and the patient asks me why I am doing so I can try to explore the meaning of the question and the associated fantasies, but I do so in the full knowledge that if they so wish they can get the answer if my reason for cancelling is due to giving a lecture because all this information is accessible. Some of my patients have the answer already to hand when they ask the question setting up perverse scenarios in the transference where the therapist – the one supposedly in the know about her life – is placed in the position of not knowing what the patient knows about her life, as I will shortly illustrate through my work with Jason. However, while not all therapists have a public profile, there is still private information that can be gleaned about all of us via the Internet – some of which is sometimes wrong – so the challenge to anonymity is a problem we all share (Gabbard, 2015).

Digital transference

What are the implications of this new landscape that exposes the analyst's private and professional life at a click of a button? Does it undermine the development of the transference? Does it threaten the analytic endeavour?

In my view the development of the transference in the context of an analytic encounter, whatever the setting, is not going to be undermined by this new external context. Nothing can undermine its development but it can alter *how* it develops. The current digital landscape provides a new context for the development of fantasy and hence of the transference. As such it has implications for our work for the following reasons:

1   It undermines the therapist's anonymity in one fell swoop and thereby short-circuits the work of representation: actual data about the therapist

dampens the patient's curiosity and reduces the tension necessary to spur the work of representation.

2   It can magnify the narcissistic imperative to know and control the object without requiring the object's consent leading to rapid escalation of perverse scenarios. This can lead to a very rapid intensification of transferential dynamics that can spin out of control as opposed to more gradually unfolding and being received by the therapist and hence contained.

3   It can accelerate sexual and aggressive impulses by providing a normalised channel for their speedy gratification (i.e. it invites acting out) that might have otherwise remained more open to interpretation and representation.

By reducing the gap between fantasy and action new technologies, as they intersect with the transference relationship, thus pose new risks for analytic work with some patients, particularly those who have borderline, narcissistic and perverse features. These individuals are more likely to use the Internet and the data about the analyst they can obtain in order to control, intrude into or triumph over the analyst. I am not referring here to scenarios where as a consequence of an enactment the therapist is actually at physical risk; rather I have in mind more mundane and yet undoubtedly intrusive forays into the therapist's personal life such as discovering details of children's names, of their schools, of divorces, of the cost of a home and so on that contribute to a concretisation of the patient's transference relationship to the therapist undermining its 'as if' quality. This is especially perilous when the psychotic part of the patient's mind is in ascendance. The greatest risk lies in how a process of reflection can be dangerously diverted off its course and threatens the viability of the work in some cases. Let me now illustrate this with a clinical vignette.

Jason

Jason was a 19-year-old young man referred because his parents had become quite concerned about his 'rages', which were sometimes intensified by alcohol but not exclusively so. He still lived at home while studying but he appeared to have grown disaffected with his studies. Consequently the parents also worried that he might drop out of university. The parents were both highly intelligent and cultured individuals who were sympathetic towards psychoanalysis as the mother had found it useful in her own lifelong battle with depression.

Jason came to see me reluctantly though he conceded that his behaviour towards his parents could be 'shocking', as he put it. He spoke with some detachment about his mother's depression and his father's felt to be 'autistic' features that he thought had impacted adversely on the family. His younger sister was described as an 'undiluted success'. He said he was attached to her but I sensed that this relationship was a very ambivalent one – on his side at least.

A notable feature of his physical presentation was that he was short in stature and seemed uneasy in his body. He told me that he had not yet had any intimate relationships of significance. He had few friends and appeared to feel safest when on his own, in the privacy of his own room and thoughts. When he spoke about others I often detected a trace of contempt as he positioned himself as more knowing and able than them. And yet I sensed that at the core he felt himself to be insufficient and that this was a primary reason for his retreat away from others.

Our work was slow to begin with. Jason came three times weekly and lay on the couch. He attended his sessions but said very little. He mostly agreed with what I said but there was a strong sense that we were not connecting. I detected a reluctance to let me into his mind. And yet I was very struck by the powerful impact his gaze had on me as he arrived and left his sessions. I often felt as if his eyes pierced right through me. As I reflected on this experience I did not feel that he was searching for something in my eyes; rather the experience was more disconcerting: it felt like he wanted to devour me with his gaze and absorb me into him.

In the early months of our work images of people breaking into houses and of 'hackers' featured in several of Jason's dreams and this added to my own sense of being 'hacked into' by his gaze. For example, a few months into the therapy he reported the following dream:

A man breaks into my parents' house. They are upstairs in their bedroom and do not hear him. He stays a long time in silence in

the reception room. He then goes through their bags in the
kitchen and takes some money but leaves everything else and
then throws the money away as he leaves the house. The next day
I come back to the house and notice the mess the burglar left
behind but my parents notice nothing. We never talk about it.

It was very hard to get Jason to associate to the dream: 'I have noth-ing to add ... I guess I was surprised by the fact that the burglar took nothing except a few £10 notes and then leaves them anyway ... maybe he did not find what he was looking for ...'

The poverty of his associations was only matched by my strong reaction to the dream. I was struck by the images of the man break-ing in and then lingering in silence without the parents noticing anything, as if the money seemed to be an afterthought, almost a cover-up for the actual reason for the break in. My own associations led me back to my countertransference and the recurrent experience of feeling that I could not negotiate an entry into Jason's mind while at the same time feeling that he was 'breaking and entering' my body though his gaze. I was intrigued too by the parents in the dream whose home is broken into and yet they know nothing of this intru-sion into their space. Jason, on the other hand, does work out what has happened but never tells them.

I eventually said to Jason that perhaps the burglar in the dream *did* find what he wanted.

Jason was perplexed and said: 'But he takes nothing in the end ...'

I said that there were many different types of 'taking' or theft that did not require actually taking anything material ... I added that the burglar in the dream had taken over the parents' space uninvited and deprived them of this knowledge and hence of their consent.

Jason then ventured, with some hesitation I noted, that these days it was easy to break into people's lives, that our tech culture encouraged this and that on balance he did not think this was a problem, though he imagined that I would see it as such.

Two weeks after this session I alerted Jason for the first time since we started the therapy that I would need to cancel a whole week the following month. I had not given Jason a reason for this break and he showed some curiosity about why I was cancelling. He said that he found it tantalising that I could cancel and give no reason for this whereas he suspected that I would want to know why he needed to miss a session. He felt this was an imbalanced relationship: it was my job to know and his not to ask.

I observed that he felt strongly about what he perceived to be my right to protect my mind and privacy from his curiosity and the requirement that in therapy he had to tell me what was on his mind.

Jason provocatively said that was what I might want but that he did not have to comply with this requirement.

I said he seemed to feel quite defiant and that he was making it clear that I had no idea what was really going on inside his mind, just like the parents in his dream a few weeks earlier who are burgled but do not know this while he knows all along but does not tell them.

Jason was silent for a long time. The silence felt stand-offish. I was mindful that I had brought back into the session a dream he had not really wanted to think about at the time he dreamt it, but that evidently *I* could not let go of. It felt as if the dream functioned in my mind as some kind of 'evidence' of a crime he was committing against the process we were both engaged in. I was quite disturbed by this realisation.

In an attempt to re-engage him I said that he was reminding me through his silence that he could keep me out, that I could not break and enter into his mind like the burglar in his dream.

Jason replied very quickly and with some force that yes, he needed to keep me out because if I found out what was in his mind I might stop seeing him.

At this stage I was somewhat taken aback by the urgency with which he had replied as if he really did feel that I might be angry about something he was withholding from me.

I said that he seemed to be very worried that I might condemn him for what he was thinking or feeling.

He quickly said: 'Not just feelings or thoughts ... actions too ...'

We were minutes away from the end of the session so I did not elaborate this further but I was left with a peculiar sense of anxiety as he left the room and surveyed me.

It took several weeks for Jason to return to the question that had been left hanging between us. I felt as if I had been left with an experience close to that in the dream he had reported: that something had been taken away from me without me knowing what it was.

The week before my impending break for which I had not given him an explanation Jason made reference to the fact that I was away the following week. I asked him how he felt about it as he clearly had it in mind.

Jason said that he had been discussing psychoanalysis with his mother and why the analyst never replied to personal questions. She told him that she had found it helpful to speak to someone who was unknown to her. He said he could not understand why all the fuss about being some blank screen ...

I said he seemed dismissive of this idea and that he wanted to know where I would be next week when I was not seeing him ...

Before I could finish my sentence Jason said: 'Turin, capital of the Piedmont region ...'

I felt jolted, not so much by the accuracy of his reply but more by the triumph that accompanied it. Rapidly the sessions of the previous months fell into place in my own mind. I revisited the dream of the burglar's double theft as I now saw it: the man breaks into the parents' private space and also steals the parents' knowledge of his intrusion so that they are broken into and duped in one feel swoop. I felt that this is what had happened between Jason and me.

I eventually said that he was now revealing the 'actions' that he had been worried about sharing with me some weeks previously for fear that I might stop seeing him.

Jason said that he had Googled me many times since he started to work with me and had noticed that I was due to give some lectures in Turin the week I had cancelled.

I said that in a part of his mind he was worried about what I would think about this, but at the same time he seemed to feel quite excited about having access to information that I had withheld from him and that he had then withheld from me.

He agreed. He said he thought the rules of therapy were 'stupid'. He could not see why I could not be straightforward about my reason for cancelling, why I turned it into a secret ... he had never liked rules 'handed from on high' that he felt were imposed on him.

Following this exchange, over the subsequent weeks, it emerged that Jason was spending long periods of time on the Internet tracking my movements, finding out where I lived and where my husband worked.

He expressed a strong interest in finding out who my children were (he imagined I had more than one child) and confessed that he had not yet managed to get any information about this. He had unearthed photos of me taken at professional events that even I was unaware existed on the Internet. I felt he played with my curiosity about which event, which photos and what else he might have discovered. It was now him looking at me 'from on high' in his omnipotent state, hiding behind a screen that paradoxically gave him the much longed for stature/potency in relation to the object while exposing his own need to hide.

Jason justified his intrusive behaviour in terms of needing to know who was helping him. He was quite resistant to any interpretations though it was also clear that he feared that I would stop the therapy. Despite this anxiety, the triumph that followed from his successful intrusiveness into me/the object was compelling and defended against anxiety. In phantasy Jason now had easy access to the parental bedroom via the Internet and he located himself in there showing no desire to move out. He used sessions to discuss his latest searches about me and he enjoyed the thought that he was unsettling me. In truth I did feel unsettled as he bulldozed through my life and somehow made it his property.

Many months later following a crisis period when Jason was confronted with failure, his narcissistic armour gave way temporarily allowing me a glimpse of his pain and fragility. He spoke of his loneliness and awareness that he was alienated from everyone, including from me. He was painfully aware of the growing gap between him and his peers and in particular the absence of a relationship. He told me that he felt that he was 'sexually deviant' and 'weird'.

However, such forays into his anxiety and vulnerability were typically quickly undermined by a retreat back into his narcissistic cocoon where he comforted himself with thoughts that he was superior to others. He began to spend increasing periods of time online, playing games and occasionally telling me that he was going to start an e-business, all of which sounded somewhat unrealistic but I sensed that he needed to see himself, and for me to see him, as a successful entrepreneur.

I became very concerned about the ease with which Jason could retreat into cybserspace and how this fuelled his omnipotence. This made it very hard for me to work with him. His invasion into my life 'remotely' was disabling the therapy as he turned a potentially help-ful space into a voyeuristic feast that was too compelling for him to relinquish.

After many months of painstaking work in the transference about his retreat into an omnipotent state of mind Jason revealed that he sometimes masturbated to a YouTube video of me discussing my work. As Jason talked to me about this it was clear that he was very excited, particularly by the way that he had managed to create a scenario where I had been recruited, unbeknownst to me, as his sexual object that he could now use as he wished whenever he wished. His masturbatory activity using images of me seemed to have acquired a compulsive quality. He joked that he had discovered through his arousal at my YouTube video that he liked 'older women' and he then started downloading pornography that involved young men with older women who were often being degraded.

My work with Jason was severely undermined by the access he had to data about me and how he used it. My invitations to think with me about what was happening in the transference, and hence in his mind, were speedily wiped out by Jason's retreat into cyberstalking. This made it exceptionally hard to find windows of opportunity for reflection.

Breaks in therapy, the end of sessions, the analyst's relative anonymity, that is those frame parameters that in the best of circumstances function as important reminders that patient and analyst are separate, were eroded in my work with Jason by the opportunities afforded in cyberspace to access me via data. In this case Jason was able to 'use' me as he wished by literally downloading me into his computer.

Enactments, of course, are the order of the day in our practices. It is not so much that they happen but how and why they do. So in one sense there is nothing new about what happened in my work with Jason. What is different, however, is how digital media that exposes personal information about the therapist alters the rate and scale of change in the transition from fantasy to action. This amplifies transference dynamics that more typically unfold over time and that are now instead transformed into a tsunami of action. For example, take the patient who entertains sexual fantasies about the therapist. Pre-Internet this patient would have needed to work at the representation in his mind of his therapist as he had no access to a tangible physical image of the therapist. Now by contrast the YouTube video of the therapist can be directly downloaded, paused, closely examined and masturbated to from the privacy of the patient's bedroom.

Clearly not all patients who search details of their therapist online are as troubled as Jason. Some such searches by patients may lend themselves to helpful analytic exploration and interpretation. However, for patients like Jason the possibilities afforded by the Internet for intrusion into the therapist's life transform the slow-burning transference process into a fire that spreads all too fast and that resists the dampening of interpretation. The seamlessness that this provides between fantasy and action can be powerfully intoxicating, fuelling the perverse structures that hold some patients together and runs counter to a core basic aim of the analytic endeavour: to represent experience.

The invasion of privacy can also mobilise strong countertransference reactions in the therapist that it is not always possible to process *in situ*. The experience of being tracked on line by a patient can be unsettling, not least because our private lives are not just our own: our families may also be exposed and we may therefore be rightly concerned about intrusion into their lives. The concreteness of the enactment can propel the therapist into action too. It is easy to become critical and rejecting of the patient or to take premature action and terminate a therapy that might be just about workable if the therapist manages her countertransference. This was my experience with Jason: while I seriously considered ending the therapy more than once the work we eventually did together confirmed that I was right in persevering. Doing so required making sense of what troubled me so deeply about his intrusion. Specifically I needed to distinguish whether my (frequent) thoughts about terminating the therapy were primarily about the impact on me of his behaviour, which left me feeling exposed and used (none of which was pleasant), or whether they signalled my apprehension of severe pathology that rendered an analytic approach unviable.

The pressure from the patient to deny that this kind of behaviour has unconscious determinants and the corresponding tendency to normalise it are common, especially among younger patients who readily dismiss the therapist's attribution of meaning to Googling details as evidence of how 'out of date' they are. My experience with Jason helped me to appreciate that it is vital to stand firm on the difference between researching details about the therapist *prior to* a therapy starting and doing this or more *during* an ongoing therapy. If technology is used in this way during the therapy this needs to be interpreted. Where technology is used to *persistently* track the therapist or to deny the reality of the end of sessions the viability of the therapy will need to be assessed. In some cases the therapy may need to be terminated. The challenge lies in engaging the patient in relinquishing the seductive pull of cyberspace where he can observe and manipulate the therapist in whichever way he chooses, and thinking and feeling with a real therapist in the real place of the consulting room.

Data as transitional phenomena

Whereas Jason used data about me so as to control and triumph over me, another patient, Karen, used it for a period of time to manage the unbearable pain of separation from me. My understanding was that for her data about me was a kind of transitional object.

The notion of transitional phenomena was used by Winnicott (1971) to describe the intermediate area of human experience between inner reality and the outside world. Winnicott focused upon how an infant moves from a sense of illusory merged omnipotence with the mother and gains a relatively firm sense of self. He was interested in how a child copes with object loss or an unresponsive social environment. Central to these concerns was his idea of transitional phenomena, which arise in the context of 'good-enough mothering', within a facilitating environment. Transitional objects, the infant's first 'not-me' possession(s), are universal and of infinite variety. Although they are actual objects (e.g. a blanket or thumb), these transitional objects are not yet perceived by the infant as having a fully external reality. They are symbolic of a third reality, a resting place that exists 'in between' subject and object – between that which is merged with the mother and that which is outside and separate. The transitional objects preserve the illusion of symbiosis with the mother thus allowing the infant the illusion that what the infant creates really exists. They mediate the inevitable disillusionment process inherent in the gradual establishment of ego boundaries as the child begins to distinguish between fantasy and fact, inner and outer, similarity and difference.

I want to suggest that some patients may use 'data' about the therapist to create an illusion of symbiosis and to manage separation anxieties elicited by the therapist's absence. Because data is 'portable' and can be accessed at all times it lends itself to being used for self-soothing and comfort just like the transitional objects of early childhood. The distinguishing feature here as opposed to the use made of data by Jason, for example, is that it is the data itself and the way it connects the patients to the therapist in her absence that is of comfort as opposed to the fantasised intrusion into the analyst's private life that creates a psychic kick that becomes compelling. Whereas the former use is a step towards the representation of the reality of separation, as I will now illustrate through my work with Karen, the latter use is an act of violence triggered by the object's separateness.

Karen

Karen was a young woman in her mid-twenties who was referred to me by her GP due to various psychosomatic complaints, the most notable of which were eczema and IBS. She had experienced the early loss of her mother after a long battle with cancer when she was twelve. Following her death Karen lived with her father and younger brother. Her father soon remarried and Karen struggled to forge a relationship with her stepmother whom she felt wanted to 'wipe' out all traces of her mother from the family house.

Although Karen had friends she kept herself somewhat remote from everyone. She lacked confidence, especially during the times when her eczema was at its worse as she felt it made her look unattractive. She had one significant relationship while at university but her partner ended it because he felt he could not manage Karen's suspiciousness of him.

She described her relationship with her mother as 'intensely close'. When she died Karen's world was shattered: she felt lost and alone. She did not feel that she could reach out to her father whom she felt had always been remote from the family. She had felt angry with him for remarrying very quickly even though she said that she could understand why he did so.

Karen came into a twice-weekly psychotherapy on the couch. Her interactions with me were tentative yet from the outset I sensed her longing for a very intense relationship with me. She responded eagerly to transference interpretations enjoying, I thought, the closeness between us that they seemed to imply rather than making use of the dynamic that they were inviting her to consider.

Breaks in the therapy were difficult for her to manage, typically manifesting in an exacerbation of her eczema. Following the first long break she returned complaining that she was not coping and expressing concern that her symptoms were worsening. She felt she needed more help and needed to see me more often. She told me anxiously that in my absence she had found herself searching for me on the Internet. She had been relieved to find that there were several entries under my name, videos and photos. She apologised for intruding on me. She was worried that I would think badly of her for doing so, but she had felt that she needed to feel close to me when I was away otherwise she would have fallen 'in pieces'.

I took up with Karen the way that she 'searched' for me on the Internet in my absence in the same way that she searched for her mother when she used to wrap herself up in her mother's scarves after her death or through sitting in what used to be her mother's favourite seat (we had discussed both of these events in earlier sessions).

Karen agreed and said that she was not looking for information about me as such, that she did not really want to know about personal details; rather she simply needed the reassurance that I existed and that there were 'traces' of me on the Internet.

I was not convinced that the discovery of personal details about me was entirely irrelevant as there were Oedipal anxieties that needed to be worked through (for example, whether I had children was of concern to her), but I was persuaded that the primary function of the data that Karen 'searched for' was to make her feel that I was still close to her, that I was alive and had not abandoned her.

For the first 18 months of the therapy breaks were managed in this way. During a particularly stressful period in her life when I had to be away she resorted to playing to herself a podcast I had made about therapy that she had managed to track down. She played it over and over again. She said that hearing my voice had induced a quasi-hypnotic trance and she had managed to calm herself down. She explained that she could not even tell me what I was talking about but the cadence of my voice and my 'European accent' as she put it, were deeply familiar and reassuring. She wished that she had a recording of her mother but besides a few videos and photos there was nothing else she could access about her.

As Karen got better she ceased to make use of the Internet to summon up my presence in her mind. She spoke eloquently of how important that phase in our work had been. She explained how the data about me that she could see and hear made her feel close to me and safe until I became a more stable attachment figure for her that she gradually took inside herself and could make use of our relationship in my actual absence.

Concluding thoughts

A key change brought about by new technologies, and one that is crucially relevant to psychoanalytic practice, is that they have completely challenged established borders of privacy. Indeed some argue that a 'systematic attack on privacy' can be observed at all levels of social life (Tylim, 2012). Sophisticated technology and powerful search engines have facilitated the availability of information as never before in the history of mankind, posing serious violations to the privacy of the psychoanalytic encounter and the centrality of the analyst's anonymity for the unfolding of the transference.

There is no doubt in my mind that these cultural changes place different demands on psychoanalytic practitioners since we cannot insulate our practice from these changes. It is not a change that affects exclusively those therapists who operate more in the public domain. It affects us all. These changes cannot be considered to be a minor modification of the setting as originally conceived of by Freud: it represents a major change. The therapist's anonymity can no longer function as a spur to the elaboration of fantasies about the therapist. This, as I have argued, does not dampen the development of the transference; rather it can amplify it all too readily. If it deprives both patient and therapist from one avenue through which to explore the patient's internal world, at the same time it provides a new one since we can understand the patient's internal world through the use they make of 'data' about the therapist. However, the patient's access to personal data imposes new strains on the therapist's own subjective experience and on the countertransference. It is therefore incumbent on individual clinicians and training institutions to systematically consider how our practice is changed so that we can manage the very particular countertransferential responses evoked by this altered setting.

Note

1   In 2014 the European Union came together to create 'The Right to Be Forgotten'. This new ruling states that search engines have to remove online information that may be a threat to 'freedom of speech'. In short, this regulation gives each person 'the right to be forgotten' by Google if he or she does not want to be traced. Because the EU ruling is still relatively new, there have been questions surrounding how effective it will be in increasing privacy.

Conclusion

Any process of major technological change generates its own mythology, not least because it comes into practice before researchers can assess its effects and implications. Consequently there is always a gap between change and its understanding. Since media theorist Marshall McLuhan's pioneering work in the 1960s, there have been numerous publications that offer a take on the impact on us of the digital age. Some argue that digital tools 'upgrade' us (Law, 2016) and foster interconnected democracy. Others, such as psychologist Sherry Turkle (1984, 1995), who studied the first generation of children raised on computers, have shifted from cautious optimism to disenchanted critique (Turkle, 2015). The neuroscientist Susan Greenfield (2014) argues that our technologies are not simply addictive: they are an existential threat. The brain, she suggests, has an 'evolutionary mandate' to adapt to its environment, and the digital world is changing at too rapid a pace for individuals, or government regulations, to keep up. Still others, such as technology writer Nicholas Carr (2010), have been hostile, describing the life of the digital mind as a 'shallows'. He argues that the Internet encourages the rapid, distracted sampling of small bits of information from many sources. Its ethic is that of the industrialist, an ethic of speed and efficiency, of optimised production and consumption.

The ancient Greeks' anxieties about the new technology of writing bear some resemblance to the anxieties that we now have about the Internet. In Plato's *Republic,* Socrates attacks poetry and argues that it has no place in the perfect state. As far as Plato was concerned poetry was a stand-in for the oral tradition of Greek thought. And yet from the perspective of today we can safely say that writing was a positive development. As with any change the perspective of time and of research is an essential part of its evaluation.

We cannot escape the fact that digital technology tethers humans and machines like never before. It is not simply that new media extend the limits of the human body and mind: they have created a new way of being-in-the-world, and a new socio-cultural environment with it, that changes how we relate to ourselves and to others and impact our experience of embodiment:

> ... technologies are not so much an extension or appendage to the human body, but are incorporated, assimilated into its very structures. The contours of human bodies are redrawn: they no longer end at the skin. (Graham, 2002: 4)

Technological mediation has truly become a defining condition of contemporary culture. Psychoanalytic theory and practice needs to be articulated within this new context. Unsurprisingly psychoanalytic theory bears the traces of the Victorian culture in which it originally evolved. Freud's developmental theories reflect the social realities of his time: a child growing up in relation to a small circle of adults who organised the child's libido in relation to those adults. The emotional universe of the child in Freud's time consisted primarily of two parents in what we would now regard as a somewhat conventional constellation that has been super-seded by varied family configurations, some facilitated by new reproduc-tive technologies, that challenge any simple conception of an Oedipal constellation.

Technology is in almost every home and in many children's bedrooms. Where once the space of the home was largely dictated and controlled by parents (who in turn were controlled by social mores), now technology opens windows to virtual exchanges in an increasingly global expanse that is not easily within the control of parents. Youth cultures exist that are not only beyond the control of parents but often also beyond their comprehen-sion. New media have indeed generated new languages too that can be hard to penetrate for the uninitiated. Take this snapshot example of an everyday conversation I witnessed between three eleven-year-old boys:

A: Got a Lapras from an egg!
B: Cp?
A: I know ... I got a 100 Electabuzz.
C: I got a Snorlaks which was 231.
B: 137cp – it sucks!

Unless you are a *Pokemon Go* fan this exchange might as well be in a foreign language. In many ways my eavesdropping was amusing but it also points to the way that digital developments have the potential to create separate areas of experience that cannot be shared equally even within the same family:

> The home has become infinitely permeable to the outside world with the result that the coherence of the culture of the nuclear family has been fragmented. (Poster, 2006: 173)

As Poster (2006) suggests, we now inhabit a constellation of family life where each member of the family inhabits a separate cultural world within the same family unit. By substituting face-to-face relating for machine mediation we have effectively reconfigured space as we alter the relation between the public and private spheres (Meyrowitz, 1985). This extends our horizons as we can travel virtually to faraway places and immerse ourselves in different cultures, but this is not without its costs at particular developmental stages.

The black mirror projects into the mind, as I have suggested in this book, and it also encourages a state of fusion that is antithetical to reflection. Desire nowadays is set up following the logic of fusion supporting immediate gratification. Anyone who has observed children or young people glued to their screens will have noticed the 'oneiric consciousness' (Poster, 2006) that is generated. The accounts of my young patients' experience of life online suggest that when in this 'machine–body' induced psychic state intentionality is suspended. Here body and mind are primed for a state of desiring located in a virtual register that operates outside of the rules of the reality principle.

In digital times a child's body is no longer primarily libidinised through his identifications with parents. The child's development nowadays unfolds in a context in which not only have childrearing practices altered, but the child's interface with machines also plays a very significant role in his embodied experience. The Victorian body of childhood, and hence the body of sexuality too, was constituted in a dynamic relation with a few other people within more clearly defined cultural contexts that limited access to sexual information and sexual stimuli. Nowadays the body of childhood bears the imprint of the technology it is tethered to and the virtual worlds that extend physical and psychic geographies for better and for worse.

Digital sexuality has a more polymorphously perverse quality. A fused machine–body desire solicits the child and prepares the body outside of the classic Oedipal paradigm. The latter operates within a context where what is lost through renunciation of the Oedipal triumph is compensated by what is gained through the process of identification and the separateness this bestows. However through new media the child's body is inscribed not only by parental projections and the identifications of the Oedipal phase but also by myriad, often part-object, ready-made identifications that operate through a complex and multifaced cyber experience suffused with sexual imagery and stimuli. What is specific to these so-called virtual identifications is that they require no psychic work – they are, in fact, more appropriately termed 'incorporations'. Perhaps the most apt image for this was the iconic UK TV (BBC) created character, the *Teletubby*, with its stomach/screen. Incorporations require no psychic movement – they are the psychic equivalent of 'staying at home' (see Chapter 3).

Just as psychic structure may be impacted on by these external trends, they are also shaping the analytic process and setting. The dominant external culture of immediate gratification, quick fixes, consumerism, normalised voyeurism and the idealisation of exposure is antithetical to some of the core tenets of the analytic enterprise. The latter is concerned with the painful work of desire, with looking inwards, with reflection as opposed to action, with bearing what we can never know – those questions that the mighty oracle Google will never be able to answer because it could not even anticipate them. The unconscious, after all, cannot be reduced to any type of algorithm.

Offering psychoanalytic psychotherapy through the medium of technology, interposing physical distance between therapist and patient, represents a significant modification of the analytic setting. As therapists we need to recognise this and speak to the patient's doubt and anxiety that what we offer may not be in their best interests. Moreover, a technology-mediated psychotherapy setting is not value-neutral: it represents an espousal of contemporary values that cannot be separated from the use of technology to promulgate lies on a vast social scale. My clinical experience has repeatedly borne out the importance of carefully tracking the patient's unconscious experience of this medium for therapy and how it impacted on their experience of me as trustworthy or not. On some occasions this has led the patient to make efforts to attend in person even against the odds. I suspect that had I not addressed the way that in offering Skype therapy I had somehow colluded with something that was not actually helpful to them, the Skype therapy would have continued but the integrity of the analytic process would have been compromised.

There are occasions when Skype therapy is 'better than nothing'. For some patients mediated therapy may be the only way they can tolerate any kind of engagement in a therapeutic process. And the therapy may be helpful. Sometimes it is a lifeline and this should not be underestimated. But it is also vital to recognise that it is not equivalent to the in-person experience. This has implications not only for the delivery of therapy but also for the training of therapists and their own training analyses. If we accept that in-person psycho-analytic therapy and its mediated application are not functionally equivalent then if we train colleagues based on a mediated experience we are training them for a somewhat different way of working (Essig, 2014). This question is not about effectiveness but about what competences are required to deliver different modes of therapy.

Psychoanalysts are now starting to offer some commentary on the broader social scale of the changes (Balick, 2013; Turkle, 2015). But mostly the contributions focus on how technology is impacting on psychoanalytic practice now that 'presence' has been separated from communication (Carlino, 2010; Russell, 2015; Scharff, 2013), and not nearly enough on how it may be impacting psychic development. In this book I have ventured in both directions to make a small contribution to a field that urgently requires concerted psychoanalytic attention. I would argue that psychoanalysis's developmental perspective and its understanding of psychosexuality and of the challenges posed by intimacy render it uniquely placed to provide some benchmarks for evaluating the relational and societal changes mediated by technology.

From the perspective of the consulting room I am all too aware that even if the concerns that drive people to seek therapeutic help have remained fairly constant over the thirty years that I have had the privilege to practise, technology does appear to have made some of these concerns more urgent, and for some people it provides compelling retreats that make feeling and thinking very hard. This is precisely because what tech-nology makes possible plays right into core anxieties about what it means to be intimate and what it means to be embodied. If it provides temporary relief from these anxieties it also invariably fails to resolve their underly-ing causes.

The 'new' thing – the gadget that creates excitement and relief as it appears to release us from an onerous or painful external or internal demand – is seldom, if ever, the solution to these 'old' internal and inter-personal problems. When we are contemptuous of the Luddite we do well to remind ourselves that the new Geek of Silicon Valley proselytises the fallacy that the 'new' is *always* better suited to our needs. An iPhone today has more technological capabilities built into it than existed in the first space shuttle. We don't need to halt the expansion of iPhone capabilities, but we do well to at least keep asking ourselves, at each juncture, whether we actually need the next new thing, and what are its implications for advancing or subverting human relationships. Digital technology should be a tool of human action, not a substitute for it.

An important lesson from psychoanalysis is precisely to be wary of the seduction of the 'new', of what we don't yet have, and to consider tech-nology in terms of how it enhances *and* impoverishes our lives. It urges us to consider its impact on our capacity to be intimate and how it may get in the way of knowing the specific nature of our desire. Without this knowledge we shrink the range of our experience to simply getting what we want: we focus on 'Delivery' and not on why we set out on a journey in the first place. Desire is what should make us want to make a journey towards the other. It should propel us to discover the geographies of other people's minds and bodies. This requires not only physical but also psychic movement, not the 'staying at home' that technology encourages (see Chapter 1).

As I finish off this book in Southern Italy, and with poor Internet connection, I am contemporaneously aware of the relief that I experience at not being easily reachable and of the comfort of knowing that, at its best, technology does make it possible to feel connected even when afar. We need to understand how to make best use of the wonders of technology and how to protect ourselves from its perilous seductions. This is an urgent question for psychologists, psychoanalysts, neuroscientists, educa-tionalists and governments. If ever there was a time that we needed inter-disciplinary thinking it is now. Ironically the interconnectivity that, at its best, the Internet facilitates makes this kind of thinking easier.

References

Aiken, M. (2016) *The Cyber Effect*. London: John Murray.

Aisenstein, M. (2015) 'Desire and its discontents', in A. Lemma and P. Lynch (eds), *Sexualities: Contemporary Psychoanalytic Perspectives*. London: Routledge.

Anderson, A. H., Newlands, A., Mullin, J., Fleming, A. M., Doherty-Sneddon, G. and Van Der Veldon, J. (1996) 'Impact of video-mediated communication on simulated service encounter', *Interacting with Computers*, 8 (2): 193–206.

Anzieu, D. (1989) *The Skin Ego*. New Haven, CT: Yale University Press.

Aron, L. (1996) *A Meeting of Minds: Mutuality in Psychoanalysis*. Hillsdale, NJ: Analytic Press.

Aulagnier, P. (1975) *La violence de l'interpretation*. Paris: Presses Universitaires de France.

Balick, A. (2013) *The Psychodynamics of Social Networking: Connected-up Instantaneous Culture and the Self*. London: Karnac Books.

Barak, A. and Suler, J. (2008) 'Reflections on the psychology and social science of cyberspace', in A. Barak (ed.), *Psychological Aspects of Cyberspace: Theory, Research, Applications*. Cambridge: Cambridge University Press, pp. 1–12.

Barale, F. and Minazzi, V. (2008) Off the beaten track: Freud, sound and music. Statement of a problem and some historico-critical notes', *International Journal of Psychoanalysis*, 89: 937–57.

Barfeld, W., Zeltzer, D., Sheridan, T. and Slater, M. (1995) Presence and performance within virtual environments', in W. Barflies and T. Furness (eds), *Virtual Environments and Advanced Interface Design*. Oxford: Oxford University Press.

Barlow, J. P. (1996) *Declaration of Independence for Cyberspace*. Online. https://www.eff.org/cyberspace-independence.

Baron, N. (2008) *Always On: Language in an Online and Mobile World*. New York: Oxford University Press.

Baudrillard, J. (1981) 'Simulacra and simulation', in Mark Poster (ed.), *Selected Writings Jean Baudrillard*. Stanford, CA: Stanford University Press, 1998.

Becker, E. (1973) *The Denial of Death*. New York: Free Press.

Beebe, B. (2004) 'Faces in relation: a case study', *Psychoanalytic Dialogues*, 14: 1–51.

Bergeret, J. (1977) 'Essai psychoanalytique sur l'activite orgasmique', *Revue française Psychanalyse*, 41: 587–609.

Bergson, H. (1988) *Matter and Memory*. New York: Zone Books.

Bessiere, K., Seay, A. and Kiesler, S. (2007) 'The Ideal Elf: identity exploration in World of Warcraft', *Cyberpsychology and Behaviour*, 10: 530–5.

Biocca, F. (1997) 'The cyborg's dilemma: progressive embodiment in virtual environments', *Journal of Computer Mediated Communications*, 3: 1–31.

Bion, W. R. (1967) *Second Thoughts: Selected Papers on Psychoanalysis*. New York: Basic Books.

Bion, W. (1970) *Attention and Interpretation*. London: Maresfield.

Birksted-Breen, D. (2009) '"Reverberation time", dreaming and the capacity to dream', *International Journal of Psychoanalysis*, 90: 35–51.

Birksted-Breen, D. (2016) *The Work of Psychoanalysis: Sexuality, Time and the Psycoanalytic Mind*. London: Routledge.

Bleger, J. (1967) 'Psycho-analysis of the psycho-analytic setting', in J. Churcher and L. Bleger (eds), *Symbiosis and Ambiguity: A Psychoanalytic Study*. London: Routledge, 2012.

Blos, P. (1967) 'The second individuation process of adolescence', *Psychoanalytic Study of the Child*, 22: 162–86.

Bohleber, W. (2010) *Destructiveness, Intersubjectivity and Trauma*. London: Karnac Books.

Bolin, A. (1994) 'Transcending and transgendering', in G. Herdt (ed.), *Third Sex, Third Gender: Beyond Sexual Dimorphism in Culture and History*. New York: Zone Books.

Brahnam, S. (2014) 'Therapeutic presence in mediated psychotherapy: the uncanny stranger in the room' in G. Riva, J. Waterworth and D. Murray (eds), *Interacting With Presence: HCI and the Sense of Presence in Computer-Mediated Environments*. Warsaw and Berlin: De Gruyter Open.

Brians, E. (2011) 'The virtual body and the strange persistence of the flesh: Deleuze, cyberspace and the posthuman', in L. Guillaume and J. Hughes (eds), *Deleuze and the Body*. Edinburgh: Edinburgh University Press.

Briggs, S. (2002) *Working With Adolescents*. London. Palgrave Macmillan.

Bronstein, C. (2009) 'Negotiating development: corporeal reality and unconscious phantasy in adolescence', *Bulletin of the British Psychoanalytical Society*, 45 (1): 17–26.

Bronstein, C. (2013) 'Finding unconscious phantasy in the session: recognizing form', *Bulletin of the British Psychoanalytical Society*, 49 (3): 16–21.

Bruce, V. (1996) 'The role of the face in communication: implication for video design', *Interacting With Computers*, 8: 166–76.

Busch, F. (1995) 'Beginning a psychoanalytic treatment: establishing an analytic frame', *Journal of the American Psychoanalytic Association*, 43: 449–68.

Califia, P. (2003) *Sex Changes: The Politics of Transgenderism*. San Francisco: Cleis Press.

Caplan, S. E. (2010) 'Theory and measurement of generalized problematic Internet use: a two-step approach', *Computers in Human Behavior*, 26: 1089–97.

Carlino, R. (2010) *Distance Psychoanalysis*. London: Karnac.

Carr, N. (2010). *The Shallows*. London: Atlantic Books.

Celenza, A. (2010) 'The analyst's need and desire', *Psychoanalytic Dialogues*, 20: 60–9.

Chartier, R. (1997) *On the Edge of the Cliff: History, Language, Practices*. Baltimore, MD: Johns Hopkins University Press.

Chesher, (1997) 'The ontology of digital domains', in D. Holmes (ed.), *Virtual Politics: Identity and Community in Cyberspace*. London: Sage.

Churcher, J. (2015) 'Privacy, telecommunications and the psychoanalytic setting', *Bulletin of the British Psychoanalytical Society*, 51 (5): 13–22.

Clark, A. (2003) *Natural Born Cyborgs: Minds Technologies and the Future of Human Intelligence*. New York: Oxford University Press.

Clark, H. H. and Wilkes-Gibbs, D. (1986) 'Referring as a collaborative process', *Cognition*, 22: 1–39.

Cohen, J. (2013). *The Private Life: Why We Remain in the Dark*. London: Granta.

Coleman, B. (2011) *Hello Avatar: The Rise of the Networked Generation*. Cambridge, MA: MIT Press.

Coleman, R. (2011) 'Be(come) your better self': self transformation and the materialization of images. In L. Guilllaume and J. Hughes (Eds). *Deleuze and the Body*. Edinburgh University Press.

Cresswell, T. (2004) *Place: A Short Introduction*. Oxford: Blackwell.

Cukor, P., Baer, L., Willis, B. S., Leahy, L., O'Laughlen, J., Murphy, M. M., Withers, M. and Martin, E. (1998) 'Use of videophones and low-cost standard telephone lines to provide a social presence in telepsychiatry', *Telemedicine Journal*, 4 (4): 313–21.

David, L. and Vaillant, G. (1998) 'Anonymity, neutrality and confidentiality in the actual methods of Sigmund Freud', *American Journal of Psychiatry*, 155: 163–71.

De Certeau, M. (1984) *The Practice of Everyday Life*. Berkeley, Los Angeles and London: University of California Press.

Deleuze, G. (1994) *Difference and Repetition*. New York: Columbia University Press.

Deleuze, G. and Guattari, F. (1987) *A Thousand Plateaus: Capitalism and Schizophrenia*, trans. Brian Massumi. Minneapolis, MN: University of Minnesota Press.

Deleuze, G. and Parnet, C. (2002) *Dialogues II*, trans H. Tomlinson and B. Habberjam. London: Continuum.

Denis, A. (1995) 'Temporality and modes of language', *International Journal of Psychoanalysis*, 76: 1109–19.

Denis, P. (2011) 'La expresión lateral de la transferencia', *La Revista de Psicoanálisis de la Asociación Psicoanalítica de Madrid*, 63: 171–89.

Dettbarn, I. (2013) 'Skype as the uncanny third', in J. S. Scharff (ed.), *Psychoanalysis Online: Mental Health, Teletherapy, and Training*. London: Karnac Books.

Digital Spy (n.d.) Online at: http://www.digitalspy.com/fun/news/a464219/75-per-cent-of-people-use-their-phone-on-the-toilet.html#~pjPpIhkBSOEIcY.

Doel, M. and Clarke, B. (1999) 'Virtual worlds: suppletion, s(ed)uction and simulacra', in M. Crang, P. Crang and J. May (eds), *Virtual Geographies*. London: Routledge.

Donnet, J. L. (2005) *La Situation Analysante*. Paris: Presses Universitaires de France.

Döring N. (2009) 'The Internet's impact on sexuality: a critical review of 15 years of research', *Computers in Human Behavior*, 25: 1089–101.

Erikson, E. (1968) *Identity*. London: Faber.

Essig, T. (2015) 'The "full training illusion" and the myth of functional equivalence', *Round Robin: Newsletter*, 30 (2).

Etchegoyen, R (1991) *The Fundamentals of Psychoanalytic Technique*. London: Karnac Books.

Fain, M. (1971) 'Prélude à la vie fantasmatique', *Revue française de psychanalyse*, 35: 291–364.

Falk, P. (1995) 'Written in the flesh', *Body & Society*, 1 (1): 95–105.

ffyche, M. and Pick, D. (2016) *Psychoanalysis in the Age of Totalitarianism*. London. Routledge.

Fiorentini, G. (2012) 'L'analisi via Internet: variazioni di setting e dinamiche transferali-controtransferali', *Rivista di Psicoanalisi*, 58 (1): 29–45.

Fisher, W. A. and Barak, A. (2000) 'Online sex shops: phenomenological, psychological, and ideological perspectives on Internet sexuality', *Cyberpsychology and Behavior*, 3: 575–89.

Flanders, S. (2009) 'On the concept of adolescent breakdown', *Bulletin of the British Psychoanalytical Society*, 45 (1): 27–34.

Fonagy, P. (2008) 'A genuinely developmental theory of sexual enjoyment and its implications for psychoanalytic technique', *Journal of the American Psychoanalytic Association*, 56: 11–36.

Fonagy, P. and Target, M. (1996) 'Playing with reality, 1: theory of mind and a normal development of psychic reality', *International Journal of Psychoanalysis*, 77: 217–233.

Fonagy, P. and Target, M. (2006) 'The mentalization focused approach to self pathology', *Journal of Personality Disorders*, 20 (6): 544–76.

Fonagy, P., Luyten, P. and Allison, E. (2015) 'Epistemic petrification and the restoration of epistemic trust: a new conceptualization of borderline personality disorder and its psychosocial treatment', *Journal of Personality Disorders*, 29 (5): 575–609.

Foucault, M. (1976) *The History of Sexuality 1*. Paris: Editions Gallimard.

Foucault, M. (1984) *The History of Sexuality 2*. Paris: Editions Gallimard.

Fraser, M., Kember, S. and Lury, C. (2005) 'Inventive Life: approaches to the New Vitalism', *Theory, Culture and Society*, 22 (1): 1–14.

Freud, A. (1936) *The Ego and the Mechanisms of Defence*. London: Karnac Books.

Freud, S. (1905) *Three Essays on the Theory of Sexuality*. [Standard Edition 7: 136–243.]

Freud, S. (1908) *Hysterical Phantasies and Their Relation to Bisexuality*. [Standard Edition 9: 159–66.]

Freud, S. (1911) *Formulations on the Two Principles of Mental Functioning*. [Standard Edition 12.]

Freud, S. (1912) *The Dynamics of Transference*. [Standard Edition 12.]

Freud, S. (1913) *On Beginning Treatment: Further Recommendations on the Technique of Psychoanalysis*. [Standard Edition 12.]

Freud, S. (1917) *Mourning and Melancholia*. [Standard Edition 14: 237–58.]

Freud, S. (1919) *Lines of Advance in Psychoanalysis*. [Standard Edition 17.]

Freud, S. (1923a) *The Infantile Genital Organization: An Interpretation into the Theory of Sexuality*. [Standard Edition 19, 1981.]

Freud, S. (1923b) *Beyond the Pleasure Principle*. [Standard Edition 18.]

Freud, S. (1923c) *The Ego and the Id*. [Standard Edition 19.]

Freud, S. (1927) *The Future of an Illusion*. [Standard Edition 12.]

Freud, S. (1930) *Civilization and Its Discontents*. [Standard Edition 21.]

Freud, S. (1939) *Moses and Monotheism: Three Essays*. London: Hogarth Press. [Standard Edition 23, 1981.]

Frosh, S. (1991) *Identity Crisis: Modernity, Psychoanalysis and the Self*. London. Palgrave Macmillan.

Gabbard, G. (2015) 'Privacy, the Self and psychoanalytic practice in the era of the Internet', *Rivista di Psicoanalisi*, LXI: 2.

Gaddini, E. (1969) 'On imitation', *International Journal of Psychoanalysis*, 50: 475–84.

Galatzer-Levy, R. M. (2012) 'Obscuring desire: a special pattern of male adolescent masturbation, Internet pornography, and the flight from meaning', *Psychoanalystic Inquiry*, 32: 480–495.

Gallagher, S. (2005) *How the Body Shapes the Mind*. Oxford: Oxford University Press.

Gamez-Guadix, M., Villa-George, F. I. and Calvete, E. (2012) 'Measurement and analysis of the cognitive-behavioral model of generalized problematic Internet use among Mexican adolescents', *Journal of Adolescence*, 35: 1581–91.

Gibbs, P. L. (2007) 'Reality in cyberspace: analysands' use of the Internet and ordinary everyday psychosis', *Psychoanalytic Review*, 94 (1): 11–38.

Gibson, W. (1984) *Neuromancer*. New York: Ace.

Giddens, A. (1991) *Modernity and Self Identity*. Cambridge: Polity.

Gill, M. (1994) 'Comment on neutrality, interpretation and therapeutic intent', Letter to the Editor, *Journal of the American Psychoanalytical Association*, 42: 681–4.

Gitelson, M. (1952) 'The emotional position of the therapists in the psychoanalytic situation', *International Journal of Psychoanalysis*, 33: 1–10.

Graham, E. L. (2002) *Representations of the Post/human: Monsters, Aliens, and Others in Popular Culture*. New Brunswick, NJ: Rutgers University Press.

Greenberg, J. (1996) 'Psychoanalytic words and psychoanalytic acts', *Contemporary Psychoanalysis*, 32: 195–203.

Greenfield, S. (2014) *Mind Change: How Digital Technologies are Leaving Their Mark on the Brain*. London: Random House.

Grosz, E. (1994) *Volatile Bodies: Toward a Corporeal Feminism*. Bloomington and Indianapolis, IN: Indiana University Press.

Guignard, F. (2014) 'Psychic development in a virtual world', in A. Lemma and L. Caparotta (eds), *Psychoanalysis in the Technoculture Era*. London: Routledge.

Guignard, S. (2008) 'Envy in Western society: today and tomorrow', in P. Roth and A. Lemma (eds), *Envy and Gratitude Revisited*. London: Karnac.

Gunkel, D. (1998) 'Virtual transcendent: cyberculture and the body', *Journal of Mass Media Ethics*, 13: 111–23.

Haag, G. (1985) 'La mère et la bébé dans les deux moities du corps', *Neuropsychiatrie de l'enfance*, 33: 107–14.

Hägglund, T. and Piha, H. (1980) 'The inner space of the body image', *Psychoanalytic Quarterly*, 49: 256–83.

Hartocollis, P. (1974) 'Origins of time: a reconstruction of the ontogenetic development of the sense of time based on object-relations theory', *Psychoanalytic Quarterly*, 43: 243–61.

Hayles, K. (1996) 'Embodied virtuality: or how to put bodies back into the picture', in M. A. Moser (ed.), *Immersed in Technology: Art and Virtual Environments*. Cambridge, MA and London: MIT Press.

Heartney, E. (2004) 'Orlan: magnificent "and" Best', in R. Durand and E. Heartney (eds) *Orlan: Carnal Art*. Paris: Flammarion.

Heidegger, M. (1962) *Being and Time*. New York: Harper & Row.

Heidegger, M. (1977) 'The question concerning technology', in *The Question Concerning Technology and Other Essays*. New York: Harper.

Holmes, D. (1997) *Virtual Politics: Identity and Community in Cyberspace*. London: Sage.

Ihde, D. (1990) *Technology and the Lifeworld: From Garden to Earth*. Bloomington and Indianapolis, IN: Indiana University Press.

Isaacs Russell, G. (2015) *Screen Relations: The Limits of Computer-Mediated Psychoanalysis and Psychotherapy*. London: Karnac Books.

Janin, C. (2015) 'Shame, hatred, and pornography: variations on an aspect of current times', *International Journal of Psychoanalysis*, 96: 1603–14.

Johnson, I. (2016) 'Paralysed patient walks again', *The Independent*, 11 August.

Kirshner, L. A. (1991) 'The concept of the self in psychoanalytic theory and its philosophical foundations', *Journal of the American Psychoanalytic Association*, 39: 157–82.

Klauber, J. (1986) *Difficulties in the Analytic Encounter*. London: Free Association Books and the Maresfiled Library.

Kohut, H. (1984) *How Does Analysis Cure?* Chicago: University of Chicago Press.

Kranzberg, M. (1986) 'Technology and history: "Kranzberg's Laws"', *Technology and Culture*, 27 (3): 544–60.

Krueger, D. (1989) *Body Self and Psychological Self*. New York: Brunner/Mazel.

Kujundzic, N. and Buschert, W. (1994) 'Instruments and the body: Sartre and Merleau-Ponty', *Research in Phenomenology*, 24: 206–15.

Lacan, J. (1977) *Ecrits*. London: Tavistock.

Langs, R. (1998) *Ground Rules in Psychotherapy and Counseling*. London: Karnac Books.

Laplanche, J. (2011) *Freud and the Sexual*. London: Unconscious in Translation.

Laufer, M. (1968) 'The body image, the function of masturbation and adolescence: problems of the ownership of the body', *Psychoanalytic Study of the Child*, 23: 14–37.

Laufer, M. (1976) 'The central masturbation fantasy, the final sexual organization, and adolescence', *Psychoanalytic Study of the Child*, 31: 297–316.

Laufer, M. and Laufer, E. (1984) *Adolescence and Developmental Breakdown*. New Haven, CT: Yale University Press.

Law, A. (2013) *Implosion: What the Web Has Really Done to Culture and Communications*. London: LID Publishing.

Law, A. (2016) *Ugraded: How The Internet Has Modernised the Human Race*. London: LID Publishing.

Leder, D. (1990) *The Absent Body*. Chicago and London: University of Chicago Press.

Lemma, A. and Levy, S. (2004) 'The impact of trauma on the psyche: internal and external processes', in S. Levy and A. Lemma (eds), *The Perversion of Loss: Psychoanalytic Perspectives on Trauma*. London: Whurr.

Lefebvre, H. (2005) *The Critique of Everyday Life*, Vol. 3. London: Verso.

Lemma, A. (2010) *Under the Skin: A Psychoanalytic Study of Body Modification*. London: Routledge.

Lemma, A. (2011) 'An order of pure decision: growing up in a virtual world and the adolescent's experience of the body', *Journal of the American Psychoanalytic Association*, 58 (4): 691–714.

Lemma, A. (2014) *Minding the Body: The Body in Psychoanalysis and Beyond*. London: Routledge.

Lemma, A. (2015a) 'Psychoanalysis in times of technoculture: some reflections on the fate of the body in virtual space', *International Journal of Psychoanalysis*, 96: 569–58.

Lemma, A. (2015b) 'The prostitute as mirror: distinguishing perverse and non-perverse use of prostitutes', in A. Lemma and P. Lynch (eds), *Sexualities: Contemporary Psychoanalytic Perspectives*. London: Routledge.

Lemma, A. and Caparrotta, L. (eds) (2014) *Psychoanalysis in the Technoculture Era*. London: Routledge.

Lemma, A. and Fonagy, P. (2013) 'A feasibility study of a psychodynamic online group intervention for depression and anxiety', *Psychoanalytic Psychology*, 30 (3): 367–80.

Lemma, A. and Lynch, P. (eds) (2015) *Sexualities: Contemporary Psychoanalytic Perspectives*. London: Routledge.

Lemma, A., Roth, A. and Pilling, S. (2008) *The Competences Required to Deliver Effective Psychoanalytic/Psychodynamic Therapy: Clinician Version*. Online at http://www.ucl.ac.uk/CORE.

Levy, S. and Inderbitzin, L. (2000) 'Suggestion and psychoanalytic technique', *Journal of the American Psychoanalytic Association*, 48 (3): 739–58.

Lim, C. and Hellard, M. (2016) 'The impact of pornography on gender-based violence, sexual health and well-being: what do we know?', *Journal of Epidemiology and Community Health*, 70 (1): 3–5.

Lingiardi, V. (2008) 'Playing with unreality: transference and computer', *International Journal of Psychoanalysis*, 89: 111–26.

Lipton, S. (1979) 'An addendum to the advantages of Freud's technique as shown in his analysis of the Rat Man', *International Journal of Psychoanalsis*, 60: 215–16.

Livingstone, S. and Smith, P. (2014) 'Annual research review: harms experienced by child users of online and mobile technologies: the nature, prevalence and management of sexual and aggressive risks in the digital age', *Journal of Child Psychology and Psychiatry*, 55 (6): 635–54.

Loewald, H. (1960) 'On the therapeutic action of psychoanalysis', *International Journal of Psychoanalsis*, 41: 16–33.

Lombard, M. and Ditton, T. (1997) 'At the heart of it all: the concept of presence', *Journal of Computer Mediated-Communication* (online), 3 (2). Available at: http://www.ascusc.org/jcmc/vol3/issue2/lombard.html.

Lombardi, R. and Pola, M. (2010) 'The body, adolescence, and psychosis', *International Journal of Psychoanalysis*, 91: 1419–44.

McLuhan, M. (1994) *Understanding Media: The Extensions of Man*. Cambridge, MA: MIT Press.

Mahler, M. and Furer, M. (1968) *On Human Symbiosis and the Vicissitudes of Individuation*. New York: International Universities Press.

Maus, M. (1992) 'Techniques of the body', in. J. Crary and S. Kwinter (eds), *Incorporations*. New York: Zone, pp. 455–77.

Meltzer, D. (1967) 'Identification and socialization in adolescents', *Contemporary Psychoanalysis*, 3: 96–103.

Meltzer, D. (2008 [1975]) *Explorations in Autism*. London: Routledge.

Merleau-Ponty, M. (1962) *The Phenomenology of Perception*. London: Routledge & Kegan Paul.

Messler Davies, J. (2013) 'My enfant terrible is twenty: a discussion of Slavin's and Gentile's retrospective reconsideration of "love in the afternoon"', *Psychoanalytic Dialogues*, 23 (2): 170–9.

Meyrowitz, J. (1985) *No Sense of Place: The Impact of Electronic Media on Social Behaviour*. New York: Oxford University Press.

Milon, A. (2005) *La Réalité Virtuelle: avec ou sans le corps*. Paris. Éditions Autrement.

Modell, A. H. (1989) 'The psychoanalytic setting as a container of multiple levels of reality: a perspective on the theory of psychoanalytic treatment', *Psychoanalytic Inquiry*, 9: 67–87.

Moss, D. (2015) 'Desire and its discontents', in A. Lemma and P. Lynch (eds), *Sexualities: Contemporary Psychoanalytic Perspectives*. London: Routledge.

O'Donnell, C. (1997) 'A nod is as good as a wink … or is it? A critical review of social psychology involved in video conferencing' (online). Available at: http://www.psy.gla.ac.uk//~steve/crvid.html.

O'Malley, C., Langton, S., Anderson, A., Doherty-Sneddon, G. and Bruce, V. (1996) 'Comparison of face-to-face and video-mediated interaction', *Interacting with Computers*, 8 (2): 177–92.

Ofcom (2013) *Children and Parents: Media Use and Attitudes Report*. London: Office of Communications.

Parsons, M. (2007) 'Raiding the inarticulate: the internal analytic setting and listening beyond countertransference', *International Journal of Psychoanalsis*, 88: 1441–56.

Pimental, K. and Teixeiria, K. (1993) *Virtual Reality: Through the New Looking Glass*. New York: McGraw-Hill.

Pomerantsev, P. (2106) 'Propagandalands', *Granta* (online). Available at: https://granta.com/why-were-post-fact/.

Poster, M. (2006) *Information Please: Culture and Politics in the Age of Digital Machines*. London: Duke University Press.

Pugh, K. (2016) 'Review of *Minding the Body: The Body in Psychoanalysis and Beyond* by Alessandra Lemma, Routledge, London, 2014', *International Journal of Psychoanalsis*. doi:10.1111/1745-8315.12503.

Riva, G. and Mantovani, F. (2014) 'Extending the self through the tools and the others: a general framework for presence and social presence in mediated interactions', in G. Riva, J. Waterworth and D. Murray (eds), *Interacting With Presence: HCI and the Sense of Presence in Computer-Mediated Environments*. Warsaw and Berlin: De Gruyter Open.

Riva, G., Waterworth, J. and Murray, D. (eds) (2014) *Interacting With Presence: HCI and the Sense of Presence in Computer-Mediated Environments*. Warsaw and Berlin: De Gruyter Open.

Riva, G., Mantovani, F., Capideville, C., Preziosa, A., Morganti, F., Villani, D., Gaggioli, A., Botella, C. and Alcaniz, N. (2007) 'Affective interactions using virtual reality: the link between presence and emotions', *Cyberpsychology and Behaviour*, 10 (1): 45–56.

Ross, M. (2005) 'Typing, doing, and being: sexuality and the Internet', *Journal of Sex Research*, 42: 342–52.

Sandler, J. (1994) 'Phantasy, defence and the representational world', *Infant Mental Health*, 15: 26–35.

Sartre, J.-P. (1970) 'The body', in S. F. Spicker (ed.), *The Philosophy of the Body*. New York: Quadrangle.

Schafer, R. (1983) *The Analytic Attitude*. London: Karnac Books sand Maresfield Library.

Scharff, J. (ed.) (2013) *Psychoanalysis Online: Mental Health, Teletherapy, and Training*. London: Karnac.

Schilder, P. (1950) *The Image and Appearance of the Human Body*. New York. International Universities Press.

Schore, A. (2000) *Affect Regulation and the Repair of the Self*. Hillsdale, NJ: Erlbaum.

Sevcikova, A. and Daneback, K. (2011) 'Anyone who wants sex? Seeking sex partners on sex-oriented contact websites', *Sexual and Relationship Therapy*, 26: 170–81.

Shapiro, T. (2008) 'Masturbation, sexuality, and adaptation: normalization in adolescence', *Journal of the American Psychoanalytic Association*, 56: 123–46.

Shaughnessy, K., Byers, S. E. and Walsh, L. (2011) 'Online sexual activity experience of heterosexual students: gender similarities and differences', *Archives of Sexual Behavior*, 40: 419–27.

Sherman, L. E., Michikyan, M. and Greenfield, P. M. (2013) 'The effects of text, audio, video, and in-person communication on bonding between friends', *Cyberpsychology: Journal of Psychosocial Research on Cyberspace*, 7 (2): 2–3.

Sony and O2 (2013) *Poll of 2000 People*. March.

Sperber, D. and Wilson, D. (1995) *Relevance: Communication and Cognition*. Oxford: Blackwell.

Stein, R. (1998a) 'The enigmatic dimension of sexual experience: the "otherness" of sexuality and primal seduction', *Psychoanalytic Quarterly*, 67: 594–25.

Stein, R. (1998b) 'The poignant, the excessive and the enigmatic in sexuality', *International Journal of Psychoanalysis*, 79: 253–68.

Steiner, J. (1993) *Psychic Retreats: Pathological Organizations in Psychotic, Neurotic and Borderline Patients*. London: Routledge.

Stiegler, B. (1998) *Technics and Time 1: The Fault of Epimetheus*. Stanford, CA: Stanford University Press.

Stone, R. A. (1996) *The War of Desire and Technology at the Close of the Mechanical Age*. Cambridge, MA: MIT Press.

Stratton, J. (1997) 'Not really desiring bodies: the rise and fall of email affairs', *Media International Australia*, 84: 28–38.

Suler, J. R. (2002) 'Identity management in cyberspace', *Journal of Applied Psychoanalytic Studies*, 4 (4): 455–9.

Suler, J. (2004) 'The online disinhibition effect', *Cyberpsychology and Behavior*, 7 (3): 321–6.

Target, M. (2015) 'A development model of sexual excitement, desire and alienation', in A. Lemma and P. Lynch (eds). *Sexualities: Contemporary Psychoanalytic Perspectives*. London: Routledge.

Træen, B., Nilsen, T. S. and Stigum, H. (2006) 'Use of pornography in traditional media and on the Internet in Norway', *Journal of Sex Research*, 43: 245–54.

Trevarthen, C. (1998) 'Intersubjectivity', in R. Wilson and F. Keil (eds), *The MIT Encyclopedia of Cognitive Science*. Cambridge, MA: MIT Press.

Tronick, E. Z. and Weinberg, M. K. (1997) 'Depressed mothers and infants: failure to form dyadic states of consciousness', in L. Murray and P. J. Cooper (eds), *Postpartum Depression and Child Development*. New York: Guilford Press.

Turkle, S. (1984) *The Second Self: Computers and the Human Spirit*. New York. Simon & Schuster.

Turkle, S. (1995) *Life on the Screen: Identity in the Age of the Internet*. New York: Simon & Schuster.

Turkle, S. (2005) 'Computer games as evocative objects: from projective screens to relational artifacts', in J. Raessens and J. Goldstein (eds), *Handbook of Computer Game Studies*. Cambridge, MA: MIT Press.

Turkle, S. (2015) *Reclaiming Conversation: The Power of Talk in a Digital Age*. New York: Penguin Press.

Tylim, I. (2012) 'The techno-body and the future of psychoanalysis', *Psychoanalytic Inquiry*, 32: 468–79.

Valentine, D. (2007) *Imagining Transgender: An Ethnography of the Category*. London: Duke University Press.

Vasseleu, C. (1997) 'Virtual bodies/virtual worlds', in D. Holmes (ed.), *Virtual Politics: Identity and Community in Cyberspace*. London. Sage.

Verhaege, P. (2011) *Love in a Time of Loneliness: Three Essays on Drive and Desire*. London: Karnac.

Villani, D., Cipresso, P. and Repetto, C. (2014) 'Coping with stress and anxiety: the role of presence in technology mediated environments', in G. Riva, J. Waterworth and D. Murray (eds), *Interacting With Presence: HCI and the Sense of Presence in Computer-Mediated Environments.* Warsaw and Berlin: De Gruyter Open.

Virilio, P. (2000a) *Polar Inertia*. London: Sage.

Virilio, P. (2000b) *The Information Bomb*. London: Verso.

Walaszewska, E. and Piskorska, A. (2012) *Relevance Theory: More Than Understanding*. Newcastle upon Tyne: Cambridge Scholars.

Winnicott, D. W. (1956) 'On transference', *International Journal of Psychoanalysis*, 37: 386–8.

Winnicott, D. W. (1966) 'Psycho-somatic illness in its positive and negative aspects', *International Journal of Psychoanalysis*, 47: 510–16.

Winnicott, D. W. (1971) *Playing and Reality*. London: Karnac Books.

Winnicott, D. W. (1972) 'Basis for self in the body', *International Journal of Child Psychotherapy*, 1: 7–16.

Wirth, W., Hofer, M. and Schramm, H. (2012) 'The role of emotional involvement and trait absorbtion in the formation of spatial presence', *Media Psychology*, 15: 19–43.

Wood, H. (2011) 'The internet and its role in the escalation of sexually compulsive behaviour', *Psychoanalytic Psychotherapy*, 25: 127–42.

Wood, H. (2013) 'The nature of the addiction in sex addiction and paraphilias', in M. Bower, R. Hale and H. Wood (eds), *Addictive States of Mind*. London. Karnac Books.

Wood, H. (2014) 'Working with problems of perversion', in A. Lemma and P. Lynch (eds), *Sexualities: Contemporary Psychoanalytic Perspectives*. London: Routledge.

Wyre, H. K. (1997) 'The body/mind dialectic within the psychoanalytic subject: Finding the analyst's voice', *American Journal of Psychoanalysis*, 57: 360–9.

Young, G. and Whitty, M. (2012) *Transcending Taboos: Moral and Psychological Examination of Cyberspace*. London: Routledge.

Žižek, S. (1997a) *Abyss of Freedom*. Ann Arbor, MI: University of Michigan Press.

Žižek, S. (1997b) *The Plague of Fantasies*. London: Verso.

Index

abstinence 105–6, 116
adolescence 5, 6, 41, 43–5, 54–67
adolescents 2, 7, 44, 47, 58, 61, 142–8
analytic setting 4, 6, 82–138
anonymity 59, 106; therapist's 114–34

becoming, (Deleuze concept of) 14, 22–3, 38, 40
black mirror 41, 45, 47–9, 54–60, 63, 137
blatancy 43–7
body as hyphen 69–70

communication, explicit 91; implicit 90–3
countertransference 36, 86, 98, 107, 124, 129, 134; somatic 93, 99, 101, 106, 113
cyberbullying 58, 90
cyberporn see pornography, internet/cyber
cybersex 31, 32, 76, 77
cybersexuality 77
cyberspace 2, 8, 13, 16–19, 21, 23–5, 31–41, 57–8, 66–71, 76–7, 92, 115, 128, 130

data 2, 67, 84, 112, 114–16, 121–2, 128–34; as transitional phenomena 116, 130–1
desire 12, 19, 46, 50, 52–3, 75, 127–8, 130; disintermediation of 65–78; sexual 31–5, 43, 47–8
disembodiment 18, 22, 72, 74–5
disinhibition, online effect 106–7
disintermediation, of the body 63; of desire 63–78

embodied presence axis 90–3; embodied setting 83–113
embodiment 4, 6, 9, 13–40, 42, 46, 69, 73, 75, 77, 92, 136

epistemic superhighway 93; trust 93–4; vigilance 94, 100

gender 37, 57
gender identity 19, 23, 26, 28, 30, 41–3, 62

identity 17–18, 23, 37–9, 41–9, 60; sexual 35, 41–9, 54–5, 60, 63, 67; trans 26
internet, effect of 2–3, 17, 19, 41, 44, 47, 116–17, 140; use/abuse of 24, 31–3, 39, 48–9, 52–77, 97, 114, 121–2, 127–9, 132–5

latency 43, 44

masturbation 47, 54–60
mobile (smart) phone 2–3, 47, 115

pleasure principle 16
pornography 47, 54; addiction 58; internet/ cyber 7, 31, 44, 48–63, 77, 128, 145
post truth 111
presence 3, 69, 71, 86–99, 107, 113–15, 133, 139
pretend mode 70–1
privacy 63, 112, 115–16, 120–9, 133–4
psychic development 14, 20, 69–77, 85, 139; dominance 38; economy 4, 40, 68; kick 131; life–experience/structure/ function 5–16, 23, 47, 54, 60, 66, 84, 114, 138; state/position 61, 111, 137, 140
psychosexuality 139

reality principle 16, 137; mixed 20; psychic 76; real 3, 7, 17, 20–1, 74, 77, 89, 107, 112; virtual 15, 17, 20–1, 33, 38, 69, 75–7, 87–8, 107, 112, 137

relationships and technology 1, 6, 37, 41, 45, 91, 140
relationships, mediated online 30, 49, 59, 61–2, 76–7, 118–19, 123
relevance axis 90–3; theory 93

scopic looting 48
sexuality 34, 36, 41–9, 56–7, 60–4, 71–5, 95, 137; adolescent 5; cyber *see* cybersexuality; digital 138; mirrored 35; virtual 35
simulation 3, 7, 14, 39
Skype 1, 66; setting 82–113, 138–9; therapy, analysis 82–3, 86–8, 90–139
somatic markers 100, 103

speed, inertia of 65, 68; of access/ availability 19, 56, 77, 122, 135; of change 5, 67–70
superego 56, 60

time of the couple 69
transference 8, 32–6, 39, 50–1, 84, 94, 98, 100, 107, 110, 114, 122; digital 114–34; erotic 35, 110, 117
transgender 30, 54, 61–2
truth 19, 26, 53–4, 71, 94, 98, 111–12, 117

virtual immediacy 38, 68, 76

work of desire 4–6, 65–7, 72, 76–7, 138